The Forgotten Romantic: Jean Paul Richter;1770-1830

Maggie Allen

CONTENTS

INTRODUCTION

The wonderful and witty German writer Jean Paul Friedrich Richter (1763-1825), although popular in his lifetime has sadly been forgotten in modern times. Whilst students of Romanticism have acknowledged the works of Goethe and Schiller, they were not likely to include those by Jean Paul, as he was not always recognised as a Romantic writer, despite making it his mission to be included in the German literary Romantic canon. There has been little research undertaken about Jean Paul for many years, although his works had always been warmly received in America.

Jean Paul Richter was writing at the turn of the 18th century and early years of the 19th century, and was very individual and unique in his style. George Stuart Collins, in the introduction to his book *Selections from the Works of Jean Paul Friedrich Richter*, stated that the other writers, and even his friend Herder, "never seem to have been in full sympathy with the trend and work of his mind."[1] Indeed, his mind was a rare and unique one that never rested. He would study everything around him, and was fully aware of the emerging trends in literature from England, France and Italy. He observed people and incorporated them, especially the women, into his novels. His style of writing included reflections of his own life, allowing him to appear in different guises in many of his novels, as well as the digressions where he could make observations about people and situations.

Although there was an interest and curiosity about him during his own time, there has remained a distinct lack of research about Jean Paul in today's academic libraries. It would appear that Jean Paul has been very much overlooked by modern day scholars, due to the popularity of the other Romantic writers. There are many questions to answer as to why he was so often omitted from the history of Romanticism. Was it because he was not really regarded as being a Romantic writer? And what ingredients were required to be recognised as a Romantic writer? These are interesting questions, and the main aim of this study is to investigate those claims.

Romanticism gave poets and writers a freedom to explore all things natural, mystical and imaginative, which leads us to question how far Jean Paul deviated from the Romantic philosophy, or indeed, if he did? Are there elements of Romanticism in his novels, or was Jean Paul just a realist? Did his writing come from any other influence or were his ideas firmly placed in the historical context? Perhaps he took the decision to deliberately oppose the wave of Romanticism and the Gothic to retain a realist viewpoint? In opposing such a trend would Jean Paul's novels actually become a catalyst for future works by writers of 'realism?

This study will investigate all elements in the novels of Jean Paul in order to answer some of these questions. It will take into account the rise of Romanticism in Europe, which was not a single, but a multiple movement being determined by social and political factors. In his book *The Romantic Revolution*, Tim Blanning confirmed that "not all Romantics – and especially not French Romantics, agreed that Romanticism had no political complexion."[3]

Referring to the French Revolution, which had inspired other European countries, the German poet Novalis commented that, "it could be transferred to the world of the imagination and administered by poets," believing that "politics should be kept out of it and that the state should be one family, bound by love."[4]

The French outcast and social critic Madame de Stael's *De Allemagne,* proved to be hugely popular as she compared the writers and their classical style in France with the Romantic output of Germany. In *Major Writings of Germaine de Stael,* she claimed "Romantic literature is the only literature still capable of being brought to perfection. Rooted in our own soil, it is the only one that can still grow and find new life."[5]

The popular publication, which quickly found favour in England (and was translated into English), was followed by other European countries who began to celebrate the Romantic approach. In pre-Victorian England, the reaction was not just to the French Revolution and European wars, but to the industrial revolution taking place.

On the literary front in England many magazines were appearing on the shelves such as the *Edinburgh Quarterly Review, Blackwood's Magazine, Gentleman's Magazine, Critical Review, English Review, Flowers of Literature* and many more, which suggested an increase of awareness in literature, as well as improved reading and literacy standards. After 1800 the magazines carried articles and examples of the works by German authors and poets.

German literature had been flooding onto the English literary scene and was very influential during the early years of the 19th century, being published in magazines such as *Blackwood's, Fraser's, The Edinburgh Review, Punch* and the *British Quarterly Review.*

Jean Paul had also found support and fame for his works in England, being promoted by Carlyle and De Quincy. George Stuart Collins claimed that Jean Paul was "introduced [in England] as early as 1821 by De Quincy; more effectively by Carlyle in his introduction to *German Romance* as well as his essays of 1827 and 1830."[6]

In the *Edinburgh Review* (1827), Carlyle wrote about the reception of German literature growing [in England] with an expanding sense of assuredness, "because it grounds itself on better knowledge, on direct study and judgement. Within the last ten years independent German readers have increased a hundredfold…we regard this revival of our intercourse after twenty years of languor or suspension as among the most remarkable and even promising features of our recent intellectual history."[7]

The English Romantic writers and poets, Keats, Shelley, Byron (*Childe Harold*), Wordsworth and Coleridge brought inspiration with their freedom of expression, adoration of the beauty of nature and the emotional world of man, much in the same way as the German writers. Both Wordsworth and Coleridge explored the ideas of everything in nature being mystical, complex and having a life source. *Christabel* is one of the best of examples by Coleridge with its uses of Gothic language and features. Germany had held a huge influence over the thoughts of Coleridge, whilst France had left its mark upon Wordsworth.

The German influence also had a later effect upon Emily Bronte who, in the early nineteenth century, had read about the German poets in *Blackwood's* magazine and attempted to emulate their style, with great effect in her fragment poems and novel *Wuthering Heights*. Her biggest influence had been Novalis (Friedrich von Hardenberg), particularly his *Hymns to the Night*[8] with their Romantic trademark of mysticism, dreams, visions and escape from the real world. Those influences could be recognised later in her novel with its cold and desolate setting of the bleak Yorkshire moors, in contrast to the German forests.

The element of Romanticism, the Gothic, had an overpowering sense of darkness and foreboding, often dealing with the uncanny, supernatural and macabre. The reading public's imagination was fired, bringing an increase in the sales of ghostly and supernatural fiction. *The Castle of Otranto* (1764) by Horace Walpole was quickly followed by Anne Radcliffe's *The Mysteries of Udolpho*, with its mountainous landscapes and cold gloomy castles, to the terrifying workings of Mary Shelley in the form of *Frankenstein*. Interestingly, it was the Gothic element of Romanticism that left its influence for us to recognise in the modern day, in the shape of Gothic architecture. Many churches had been built in the Gothic style and can often bring a chill or two when visited, and even Tennyson's father "adorned his rectory with Gothic detail."[9]

One of the main devices to be found in the novels of Jean Paul that marked out his individuality was in the use of humour. He was very fond of adopting the eighteenth century tradition of satire, which he employed to great effect when taking aim at the absurdity of people and the situations they found themselves in. It was the smaller things in life, the absurdity of human nature that captured his attention and brought a wry smile to his face. Although it could imply contempt, in the hands of Jean Paul it not only alerted the reader to the injustice and immorality of situations, but to their absurdity too. The social institutions did not escape his keen wit either, as he highlighted our attention to situations, and environments, contrasting the fictional or fantastic with the real. His love of God and of nature were his abiding passions.

Jean Paul's novel writing approach appeared to be in phases and his novels *Selections from the Devils Papers, and The Greenland Lawsuits* (1790), could be classed as bitter satire. After the vision he had of his own death, Jean Paul, or Johann Paul Friedrich (Fritz) as he was known, changed his first name to Jean, with the

French spelling, after Jean Jacques Rousseau, who he had greatly admired. His second phase and novels, included *The Invisible Lodge*, *Maria Wutz*, and *Flower, Fruit and Thorn Pieces*, and his greatest epic; *Titan*.

Jean Paul had developed into a great thinker, he was aware of the philosophies and ideologies of the day, and their authors, and prepared his own version of aesthetic theories in *Horn of Oberon: Preschool of Aesthetics*, which presented a fuller image of him as writer and poet.

The war had a profound effect upon Jean Paul, particularly the Battle of Jena. He attempted to cheer up the Germans by once again writing wit, only injected with warmth and humour, which could have been described as sentimental satire, and which formed his third phase. They were a humorous rendition of everyday life and people in 18th century Germany, providing insights into the motives and notions of his characters, their settings and problems. These novels were known as; *Dr Katzenberger's Badereise* (2 vols) and *Dr Katzenberger's Journey to the Spa.*

The novels all contained aspects of contrast and dualism; people, situations, life and death, deception and regret, the past, future, happiness and the waste of sadness, were all inter-woven themes in his writings. He was a faithful admirer of Rousseau and his influence can be seen in the works of Jean Paul. He often adopted digression and complications in his narrative, and had been identified with Lawrence Sterne because of that, but the unexpected aspect in all of them was the humour that ran through them. Jean Paul was a unique writer in that respect and it is that uniqueness that marked him out as an author who should be resurrected and respected.

An essential aspect to all the works of Jean Paul was that of nature and God. His obsession with the immortality of the soul was a regular feature, providing a spiritual element and poetic aesthetic, which was also adopted by other Romantic writers and poets, but the questions about God and mortality had affected Jean Paul for many years, following a dream he had, in his youth, about his own death. Dreams, visions, and self-confrontation via the doppelganger, Jean Paul's own invented term, were features which occurred regularly in the novels.

This study will question, if he did reject the Romantic influence, through a closer examination of his writings. It will be an interesting journey to trace the light and dark aspects of character and plot alongside the fantastic and grotesque images created with such a black wit. Initially, we are tempted to believe that Richter did employ Gothic elements, but did he just use them as a device to ridicule the influence he rejected? A closer, psychological examination of his narrative structure will reveal the truth.

Apart from a psychological consideration of the theme of humour, its roots will be traced in order to see how similar themes were employed in literature in Germany and Europe. It will also be interesting to compare the similarities of English writers who adopted the use of satire and humour during that period, such as, Tobias Smollett, Laurence Stern and Oliver Goldsmith.

According to the *Encyclopedia Britannica*, "The 18th century was prolific in the creation of kind-hearted humorists, most notably (in the UK) Joseph Addison and Sir Richard Steel's *Sir Roger De Coverley*, Henry Fielding's *Parson Adams*, Oliver Goldsmith's *Vicar of Wakefield* and Laurence Stern's *Tristram Shandy*." The Encyclopaedia defines the use of humour: "at its best it preserved a fine and difficult balance and a comprehensive conception of man and nature."[10]

The move towards social stability and national security in Germany during the 18th century affected how novelists used humour in their works. We can see this in the novels of Jean Paul as he took aim at the social, political and religious institutions of German life.

Jean Paul's own German background will be the focus of much of the study, as it was his homeland and where his novels were penned. The era of Romanticism in Europe and the literary history of Germany, were all very relevant to this study, as were the uses of humour, and even the psychological undercurrents. However, as Bayard Quincy Morgan pointed out, the Romantic Movement "proved to be a turning point in the culture of Europe, where some of the greatest writers of the age were only partly committed to its ideals, but in such a way that their exact position within the Romantic ideology remains impossible to pin down. For these and other reasons, there can be no simple, pithy definition of the term Romanticism."[11]

The conclusion of this study will provide evidence that will identify the true nature of Richter and his work as the 'Romantic,' the 'Realist,' or perhaps as a true original? His style was often a difficult one for his readers to interpret with its discordant and dualistic opposites. His world of mirrors will reflect, by closer examination, how this study will reach the categorization of such a complicated writer.

End notes:

1. Collins, George Stuart, *Selections from the Works of Jean Paul Richter* (New York: Cincinatti: Chicago: American Book Company, 1898), p.12

2. Furst, Lilian, *Romanticism in Perspective* (London: MacMillan, 1969), p.36

3. Blanning, Tim, *The Romantic Revolution* (London: Weidenfeld & Nicolson, 2010), p.54

4. Fitzgerald, Penelope, *The Blue Flower* (London: Flamingo, 1996), p.61

5. Folkenflik, Vivian, *Major Writings of Germaine de Stael* (New York: Columbia University, 1987), p.302

6. Collins, p.13

7. Stockley, V, German Literature as Known in England 1750-1800 (London: George Routledge, 1929), p., 13

8. Prokofieff, Segio O, (Ed), *Hymns to the Night & Spiritual Songs* (London: Temple Lodge, 2001)

9. Kenneth Clarke, *The Gothic Revival* (London: John Murray, 1962), p.111

10. *Encyclopedia Britannica, vol: 2* (UK: Encyclopedia Britannica, 1973), p.841

11. Morgan, Bayard Quincy & Hohfeld, *German Literature in British Magazines 1750- 1860* (Madison, Wisconsin: University of Wisconsin Press, 1949), p.52

Chapter One:

Jean Paul

According to Thomas Carlyle, in his essay about Jean Paul, "the biography of so distinguished a person could scarcely fail to be interesting."[1] He later stated that "Germany has long loved him; to England also he must, one day, become known; for a man of this magnitude belongs not to one people, but to the world."[2] William Cleaver Wilkinson also described Jean Paul with admiration, as having, "the largest, softest, most loving heart in literature – heart pure, too, of the purest – was Richter, Richter the unique, the only."[3]

To write the biography of a person's life may be to record date of birth and death with occupation, and personal life, alongside major achievements, in the case of a writer, his novels. However, when considering the life of Jean Paul, the biographer needed to be prepared, and aware of, the frequent twists and turns, the uniqueness of temperament, the workings of his mind which switched from humour to theology, diverging into philosophy and poetry, and then there was his interest in education. All those aspects can be found in his life and works, and will illustrate whether it will be possible to place Jean Paul into the sphere of Romanticism or Realism.

One of the greatest influences in the life of Jean Paul had been Rousseau, whose philosophies had laid the foundation for all Jean Paul's thoughts and works. Lytton Strachey referred to him as "among those quick, strong, fiery people of the eighteenth century, he belonged to another world – to the new world of self-consciousness, and doubt, and hesitation, of mysterious melancholy and quiet intimate delights, of long reflexions amid the solitudes of Nature, of infinite introspections amid the solitudes of the heart."[4] That description, aimed at Rousseau, could have fitted Jean Paul suitably.

There can be no doubt that, through the images we have of him and his life, it would not be unreasonable to class him as a Romantic figure, emerging from the beautiful and natural surroundings of the Fichtelgebirge, which would have been the ideal surrounding for any poet or writer of Romanticism. Casey, however, argued that Jean Paul "idealized what was in reality frequently a wretched existence, not only because of the poverty, and subservient position of teachers and parsons but often because of their own narrowness [and that] in the more idyllic works the reader is made aware of the underlying realities. [But], he admits, that the works include many "idyllic scenes of childhood, lamplight, firelight, [and] Christmas, and that he "often mocks himself as a domestic snail, speaking of his inglenook disposition and his spiritual nest making."[5]

Life for Jean Paul was multifaceted, interesting, full of observation and deep contemplation, and although there have been many biographies written about the life of Jean Paul, since his death in 1825, the account given by Eliza Buckminster Lee is an extensive translated version. She gave a complete picture of his life, with information taken from his family and authentic documents. It was not a brief encounter, but a real and true documentary about the growth of a unique and sensitive writer. Buckminster Lee managed to get beneath the skin and into the mind of Jean Paul, so that we travel through his life, alongside his up's and the frequent down's. We are given a picture of the man and the artist at work. Her descriptions are vivid and real, as she paints a portrait of the man and his background, his family and the people he came into contact with.

In the Preface to the biography she commented upon the vast wealth of information collected, which caused problems in selecting the most appropriate and essential details that would be required for students of Richter. She termed these details, "gems worthy of the purest gold, and the richest pattern."[6]

The high, mountainous area of Germany, the Fichtelgebirge, where Jean Paul was born, was described by Buckminster Lee in an extensive, elaborate and artistic way, with each detail giving an atmosphere and rural charm to the portrait. She commented about the beauty and nature of the Fichtelgebirge, and how, "it would be impossible for a poet with so keen a susceptibility to all impressions as Richter, to be born under such influences and to pass his youth just within the threshold of a region so filled with romance, without its having a powerful, but perhaps secret influence upon the whole man, and upon the character of his genius and writings."[7]

Those comments, written shortly after the death of Jean Paul, indicated that the theme of his writings followed that of Romanticism, adding weight to the question of categorization, which this study aims to answer. Scholars and critics have, over time, attempted to categorize the work of Jean Paul, but without offering any firm conclusions.

In accordance with nature, Jean Paul was born on the first day of Spring, March 21st 1763, as the "robin-redbreast, the crane, the red-hammer, snipes and woodcocks,"[8] all made their way into a new world. His father, John Christian Christopher, was a teacher, and his mother, Sophia Rosina, was the daughter of a cloth-weaver, together with his grandfather, they were a very close family whose influences remained throughout the life of Jean Paul. The death of his grandfather left a lasting impression and Jean Paul commented, "Pious grandfather! Often have I thought of thy cold, blessing hand when fate has led me out of the dark into brighter hours; and I needed to hold fast my faith in thy blessing, in this world, penetrated, governed and animated by wonders and spirits."[9]

Jean Paul's father had been a talented musician, although he had studied Theology at Jena and Erlangen. The memoirs of Jean Paul recalled the playing of the piano and brass instruments in the Catholic Church of Bayreuth, where his father would enchant the congregation with an "exhibition of that holy power of music, the tones of which even to this day elevate and sanctify souls in the Catholic Church."[10] But it was the personality of Jean Paul's father which left a lasting legacy through his wit and jests and amusing anecdotes, which accompanied him through life.

The influence of his father's personality could be recognised in Jean Paul's own views of the world, where wit was never far away from his observations of people and situations. Jean Paul's account displays some regret about his father's musical inclination in favour of the Church. "Indeed, the Church, according to the opinion of my grandparents, was then the provision-ship and air-balloon, and the needy son of the Muses sought to run into the quiet haven of the pulpit."[11]

The admiration Jean Paul had for his father, was echoed with the words, "eloquence, the prosaic, but near neighbour to Poetry, dwelt in my father's heart."[12]

It was the appointment of his father as Pastor in Joditz which began to alter the lives of Jean Paul and his parents. Buckminster Lee claimed that it was in those idyllic years that [Jean Paul] "received impressions which would follow him through life and influence all his works. Never is he so much at home in his works, as in the little village parsonage and church...the village festivals, the church consecrations, are all dear to his deeply religious spirit."[13]

During those years Jean Paul developed a love for learning, reading, painting, music, and the start of his interest in philosophy. He claimed, "never shall I forget, that which I have never yet related to human being, - the inward experience of the birth of self-consciousness…that inward consciousness. *I am Me* came like a flash of lightening from Heaven and has remained ever since. Then was my existence conscious of itself, and forever."[14]

On the negative side Jean Paul admitted to his fear of ghosts and the spirit world. His father had given him a lot of information about his own spiritual experiences and visions, but confirmed to the young Jean Paul that his beliefs acted as a shield against any harm. As an imaginative child these recollections made him tremble before the *invisible* world."[15] Jean Paul confessed to his fear of ghosts in the daytime but sensed the church to be "shadowy, silent and listening…" and how he had ran so fast into the church and back when returning his father's Bible to the sacristy after a funeral, as if he had "the world of spirits at one's heels."[16]

After the death of his father Jean Paul moved to a town called Schwarzenbach-sur-la-Saale, where he was formally taught the piano. At the same time he became interested in the literature of the day. On his bookshelves he had only a copy of Schiller's *Amenian*. From reading books, obtained from wherever he could find them, Jean Paul formulated his own philosophy of 'seeing and hearing,' as opposed to writing and speaking… "sun, moon, and stars, and all the appearances in nature, touched him nearly, and were all dear to him. The ever-changing clouds upon the Fichtelgebirg were not watched merely with the eye of a poet or painter; he was the listener and interpreter of Nature in all her relations with man, and his acute and deep observation and knowledge are expressed in many humorous and many serious aphorisms."[17]

During his youth Jean Paul began to question his faith. The questions followed him through his life and appeared in his works. "He continued in his quest for knowledge and the truth, reading philosophical theology, natural history, medicine, poetry and juris prudence."[18] The extent of his research led to the question of whether Jean Paul should have followed the path of a philosopher rather than a poet.

Buckminster Lee commented that the youth of Jean Paul and his scientific study took place against the background of an emerging literary period known as the *Werther* period, which was the brainchild of Goethe, and followed the ideals of the Enlightenment. The effects of the period resulted in a literary wave of sentimentality.

Jean Paul was more concerned with his own research rather than the display of such feelings as unleashed by Goethe. He produced a self-made book which contained barbed, but witty references to Goethe, "Goethe is such a sketcher. He touches the sympathising heart at every point. Has not all Germany wept with him?"[19]

In 1781 Jean Paul followed in his father's footsteps to study for a degree in theological studies, at Leipzig, with the aim of, afterwards, joining the clergy. He felt it was the correct thing to do for his mother, who, following the death of his father had very little money and was facing her own battles in court to claim an inheritance from her own family. Jean Paul was aware of the struggles faced by his mother, and was trying in his own way to help. The resentment he felt, silently emerged in a letter to a friend, in which he claimed, "to study for what one does not love; that is, to contend with ennui, weariness, and disgust, for a good that we do not desire; to lavish the talent, that we feel is created for something else, in vain, on a subject where we fear that we cannot succeed, is to withdraw so much power from one where we could make progress." [20]

Jean Paul's period of despair led him to an unexpected literary development, changing his reading habits from philosophical writings to "the witty, elegant, imaginative authors [reading] the French books rather than German, [including] the wit of Voltaire, the eloquence of Rousseau, the ornamented style of Helvetius, and the ingenious remarks of Toussaint…" [21] Of the English writers, Jean Paul stated that he "read Pope – he delights me; so does Young. There is nothing more splendid in the English language! I learn it now chiefly to read that excellent weekly paper, the Spectator, of which we have in Germany but a miserable translation."[22]

With poverty, debt, and concern for his mother hanging over him, Jean Paul decided to write his first manuscript, in a bid to earn money. He wrote *Eulogy of Stupidity* (*Die Lob der Dummheit*), which failed to be published, prompting him to write the *Greenland Lawsuits*, which were a "collection of moral, satirical (but bitter) sketches upon life, under the titles of 'literature,' theology,' family pride, and 'women and fops."[23]

When Jean Paul had found a publisher his success was marred by the death of his brother. He tried to write more books with wit at the heart of them, but his own life was in complete contrast, dark and depressing. He began to alter his appearance in order to save money, "that his convenience, health and poverty obliged him to wear."[24]

Having completed and published his second volume of *Greenland Lawsuits*, he began working on his third novel, *Selections from the Papers of the Devil.* He was fascinated that "without characters, without action of any kind, he could write satires that would interest the reading public."[25]

Although he could not find an editor or publisher for his third novel, Jean Paul continued to write articles and essays for magazines, but discovered that readers did not have any interest in satire. In a comical episode Jean Paul disguised himself to escape his debtors, fleeing back to the safety of Hof and his mother. Even in his last days, Buckminster Lee informed us, "Jean Paul loved to relate his flight, as he called it, out of Leipzig."[26]

Returning to his home he turned to poetry, observing nature, the people, his books, and his inner world of thoughts, to become "the poet of the poor."[27]

Adam von Oerthel, Jean Paul's friend, had returned from Leipzig with the offer of a new home and job teaching French to his younger brother. Paul was not very happy in the new situation as Adam became ill and died, leaving Jean Paul to return home once again.

The deaths of Adam and his own brother had made a deep impact upon Jean Paul, and he began to contemplate the suffering of humanity. He read Klopstock's *Ode to Death* which made him think differently and create an alternate way of thinking. He poured his thoughts out in a book of devotion in which "he analysed his own soul, and entered upon the noble effort to acquire for himself and others, the exalted hopes, and the sure trust in God, and in human virtue, that is not shut out from the poorest and most limited relations of human life."[28]

Herder, (1744-1803) one of the most prolific authors and philosophers of the time, and who had written passionately about the place of literature for the future of Germany, was the person to who Jean Paul turned, although it was Caroline, the wife of Herder, who first read Jean Paul's manuscript, and was impressed by it. It was the start of a friendship that lasted throughout their lives. Buckminster Lee stated that "it was a prophetic assurance that from the German women he should receive through life, the richest rewards of fame."[29]

On his return to Hof, Jean Paul also returned to his natural appearance, in accordance with the changes in his literary habits, from satirical and witty author to serious poet. He became a regular and popular visitor to his many friends and neighbours, and joined in all the social activities, often playing the harpsichord and piano, pouring out "all the emotions, images, and dreams of his soul, without the timidity that he had always felt at expressing them in words, and excited or melted his hearers with his own emotions…he would break off suddenly, and begin the most humorous stories of his future life; of his journeys, his wife, his children (which were always three); then he would prophesy, but always with whimsical effect, what a great man he would be – how people would come from all places to see him, and princes and princesses would envy us the pleasure of his society." [30]

He may not have achieved royal status, or endorsement, but he was always well loved and regarded by all who knew him or had read his works.

In 1790 Jean Paul began teaching in school. They were some of the happiest days of his life, in which he encouraged the children to develop in all the aspects of the curriculum, but always reminded them about the "ever-present thought of God and immortality."[31] The book, *Levana,* gave an account of Jean Paul's forward-thinking approach to education and the creativity aspect that he considered important, his influence taken from his idol, Rousseau.

Jean Paul was very popular with the ladies, Buckminster Lee noted the names, Caroline, Helena, Frederica, and Amonè, who was later to marry Jean Paul's friend, Otto. Although he was popular with his circle of female admirers, Jean Paul found it difficult to find his one true love. He wrote, "I ask not the most beautiful *person,* but for the most beautiful heart, in that I can overlook blemishes, but in this, none…there can be but one beloved, that can forget all for thee, and give thee every minute, every glance, every joy, every beating of the pulse, and say to thee, [that] we have chosen each other from the whole world."[32] Although he met many ladies, he found it difficult to find his ideal. To one of his admirers he sent an essay entitled, *Essay Upon the continuance of the Soul and its Consciousness.*

That essay provided the foundation and spring-board for the novel, *Kampaner Thal*. Buckminster Lee pointed out that his further works were "henceforth created to elevate in happiness, to soothe and cheer in sorrow [but] satire remained among his lighter weapons, but he took from it the bitterness of scorn, and henceforth his vinegar was made from honey."[33]

Jean Paul asked his friend Christian Otto to read his new novel, *History of the Contented little Schoolmaster Maria Wuz,* which contained references to his teaching career, containing more of the sentimental, as he explored human nature, than was usually found in his works. He referred to it as, " the bridge over which he passed from the vinegar fabric where he had worked nineteen years, when he closed the door to satire, and opened it to all that loved and rejoiced and wept with human nature."[34]

Jean Paul's next novel was *The Invisible Lodge*, a romance, although education and his own life experiences are woven into the theme. He had sent the manuscript to a publisher called Hofrath Moritz, who claimed, when he saw the manuscript, "it is Goethe, Herder or Wieland... [but] it was above Goethe – it was something wholly new."[35] With success and new found wealth, Jean Paul's turned to help his mother, who was very proud of her son. He then set to work on *The Hesperus*, which according to Buckminster Lee was, "the work by which the author has been best known, out of Germany.

In Germany, Titan is THE WORK, the GREAT WORK of Jean Paul, [but] Buckminster Lee admitted, the story of *Hesperus* "is so confused, that probably many persons have read and admired the book, without even getting a clear idea of its story."[36]

In 1794 Jean Paul returned again to teaching, and also began writing his next novel, *Quintus Fixlien*, the theme of which represented the poor in society. It was at that time he met the wealthy Jewish Emanuel in Bayreuth, where he was pleased to discover his books being read and appreciated.

He worked continually and produced *Blumen-Frucht-Und-Dôrnenstukke* (*Flower, Fruit and Thorn Pieces*), a collection of pieces, and translated by Madame de Stael, which brought fame for Jean Paul outside of Germany. But in Germany Jean Paul's name was being talked about alongside Goethe and Schiller, Wieland and Herder.

When Jean Paul travelled to Jena he was welcomed by Wieland and Herder, but did not get the same reception from Goethe and Schiller. According to Buckminster Lee "Goethe's contempt for Jean Paul is shown through his letters to Schiller."[37] Ironically, Jean Paul, in a letter to Otto stated, "who would believe that the three watch-towers of our literature avoid and dislike each other."[38] Upon visiting Goethe and hearing him read some of his poetry, Jean Paul felt differently. Goethe gave him a letter of introduction to Schiller.

After visiting Schiller, Jean Paul had formed quite an opinion about the famous writer and friend of Goethe's. He referred to Schiller as "stony…from whom, as from a precipice, all strangers spring back. His form is worn, severely powerful, but angular. He is full of sharp cutting power, but without love."[39] Schiller may have appeared unapproachable but he offered Jean Paul the opportunity to contribute some of his work to the periodical, *The Horen.*

During the following few years Jean Paul worked on the *Kampaner Thal* (*Immortality of the Soul*), which was more serious and poetic than his other works. It was just after that, about 1797, time he learned of his mother's death. Jean Paul took his brother Samuel to Leipzig, but Samuel got into bad company and fled. Jean Paul continued to support his brother, paying a yearly allowance through his friend Otto. Samuel died later in a military hospital in Silesia.

Jean Paul returned to Weimar and his friends, where he met Fichte, and the Schlegel brothers. From the philosophy of Fichte, Jean Paul returned to his thoughts of earlier years about the state of humanity. With Herder and Jacobi, Jean Paul planned to publish a journal called *Aurora,* but age and ill-health of Jacobi and Herder meant that the project had to be abandoned. Jean Paul re-wrote *Selections from the Devil's Papers.* Buckminster Lee quoted a critic of the time who claimed, "it [was] one of the works of the author that gives the most lucid explanation of the being and nature of the poet, and places poetical influences in the clearest light."[40]

In 1799 Jean Paul completed *Titan, as well as* the *Eulogy of Charlotte Corday. Clavis Fichtiana* was one of his most celebrated works, due to the popularity of Fichte, and which set him apart from Goethe and Schiller. In 1800 he travelled to Berlin where he decided to settle and marry Caroline Meyer. They had a daughter. In 1803 Jean Paul wrote the *Flegeljahre,* and they moved to Cobourg, where Caroline gave birth to a son, happiness contrasted with the sadness, when Jean Paul's close friend Herder, died.

Dorothy Berger commented that "Jean Paul had changed during his married life. He was no longer the ethereal youth adored by young girls and Romantic women; he was now rather fat. He lived like a bachelor, thus giving his wife considerable anxiety. She tormented him occasionally with her jealousy, her complete lack of humour, and her idea about the upbringing and education of their children."[41]

Buckminster Lee did not reflect upon this but did comment that Jean Paul liked to journey to different places alone. Perhaps it was a case of the artist and acute observer preferring solitude to distraction, as he contemplated his future essays and novels.

In 1804 Jean Paul wrote the novel *Walt and Vult* or *The Twins*, Caroline gave birth to another daughter and they moved to Bayreuth. It was there, with the beautiful vision of surrounding nature that Jean Paul wrote his critical and scientific, *Introduction to Aesthetics*. He wrote many articles and essays in a bid to earn money as the country was facing war.

1807 was a turning point in German history with the Battle of Jena and take over by Napoleon. Jean Paul's *Levana* was finally published, but he felt the need and responsibility to cheer up the German readers from the state of depression the country was languishing in. He returned to using humour and in 1809 wrote *Dr. Katzenburger's Journey to a Spa,* and *Army Chaplain Schmelzle's Journey to Flätz.*

The German author E.T.A. Hoffmann in 1811, visited Jean Paul, "who subsequently assisted Hoffmann in launching his career."[42] They had similar interests and music was a great passion for them both. It played a large part in the novels written by Hoffmann. Two years later, 1813, and Jean Paul wrote *Reminiscences of the Best Hours of Life for the Hour of Death,* and made several journeys, often to Heidelberg to see his son, who was causing some concern for Jean Paul.

His son returned home and died shortly afterwards, which had a deep and significant impact upon Jean Paul. His own health began to suffer and his eyesight became affected, but he continued to write and produced *The Life of Fibel.* According to Buckminster Lee, the Germans regarded the author more successful in his later years than in his earlier works. They found his humorous works to be more artistic and perfect, as works of art, than his serious pieces.

Although he was often philosophical and serious, humour was more suited to him. He strove for perfection in works, but his success was created largely by his portraits of the everyday people and situations that the German reading public could relate to.

The life-time success of Jean Paul led to him receiving an Honorary Doctor's degree from Heidelberg University. His eye-sight continued to fail, but in 1820 he produced *The Comet,* a novel full of laughter and tears. He could no longer continue to write but he dictated to his friend Otto his last novel, which was *Selena,* based upon his theory of life after death. Jean Paul died in 1825, after ensuring it was ready for publishing. His friend Otto followed him to the grave.

In her conclusion Buckminster Lee marked the distinction between Richter and Goethe as being from "opposite schools of literature[43] pointing out their very different cultural backgrounds, as well as the differences in their character and works. She observed that "Richter's life may be divided into three epochs, and his works into three corresponding divisions. The first, that of pure satire, terminated with the writing of the Contented Schoolmaster…his French and English led him to Pope, Shaftesbury, Swift, Rabelais, and the encyclopaedists. He wrote only satires. To give interest to his essays, which were without any poetical or dramatic charm, he embellished them with illustrations, anecdotes, proverbs, and quaint expressions, developing what Carlyle termed his "claptrap manner."[44]

Buckminster Lee also commented upon the contrast between the humorous and the serious, which "never ceased, but that it was humour that usually won, but having changed from the bitter content to a humour of love, pouring the balm of a sympathising spirit over the wounds of humanity, and that it was the humour of Jean Paul that made him so beloved by the Germans.[45]

In his *Preface* to *Quintus Fixlein*, Jean Paul explained the thoughts behind his work, "that I may show to the whole earth, that we ought to value little joys more than great ones…Can I accomplish this, I shall, by means of my book, bring up for posterity a race of men finding refreshment in all things…You perceive my drift is, that man may become a little tailor-bird, which, not amidst the crashing boughs of the storm-tossed, roaring, immeasurable tree of life, but upon one of its leaves, sews itself a nest together, and there lies snug."[46] Embroidered together with many examples of his philosophy interwoven into his text, Jean Paul gave his reasons for being happy.

Throughout his books, Jean Paul had the same philosophy of contrasting the real with the ideal. For him, chasing the ideal, would meet with confusion and disappointment, which reflected upon his own life in many ways. He would always return to the simplicity of nature and life, his observations of humanity, and which led to his own philosophy of sentimentalism, which was a form of emotion but coupled with humour; a type of warmth which radiated throughout his works, using words that his countrymen could empathise with.

Buckminster Lee commented about the strained relationship between Jean Paul and Goethe at their early meetings, and believed that Goethe could have been a big help to Jean Paul. Although Jean Paul had enormous respect for Goethe, he was a very different and original writer. Jean Paul had his own unique style that with outside interference or pressure, may have altered the course of his life and success. Buckminster Lee stated that Jean Paul was,

"like a solitary sage [looking] out from his hermitage upon the ever-swelling and rushing waves of the literature and politics of that remarkable period in which he lived. Unmoved by its passions, still and calm, he was like a holy prophet of its issue; glowing for freedom, truth and the happiness of man, yet never failing in the clearness of his understanding, or the firmness of his will. Full of scorn and hatred of all servility and all tyranny, yet ever free from the folly and madness of enthusiasm."[47]

Buckminster Lee's final words were a fitting tribute to the unique individual style of Jean Paul, who worked against the backdrop of a literary revolution, political situations and personal struggles, to define his own beliefs and individuality.

He opened up his heart and mind to remain faithful to people and nature. Carlyle offered his thoughts about Jean Paul, that he "had in him that which does not die; that Beauty and Earnestness of soul, that spirit of humanity, of Love and mild Wisdom, over which the vicissitudes of mode have no sway. This is that excellence of the inmost nature which alone confers immortality on writings…"[48]

End Notes

1. Carlyle Thomas, *Critical & Miscellaneous Essays: Jean Paul Friedrich Richter – state of German Literature – Life & Writings of Werner.* (New York: John B Alden, 1885), p.9
2. Carlyle, p.27
3. Wilkinson, William Cleaver, *Classic German Course in English* (New York: Chautauqua Press, 1891), p.122
4. Blanning Tim, *The Romantic Revolution* (London: Orion Books, 2010), p.9
5. Casey, Timothy, J, *Jean Paul: A Reader* (Baltimore & London: The John Hopkins University Press, 1992), p.9
6. Lee, Buckminster Eliza, *Life of Jean Paul Frederic Richter,* vol.1, (U.S.A, Boston: Charles C. Little & James Brown, 1842), Preface.
7. Lee, p.10
8. ibid, p.11
9. ibid, p.17
10. ibid, p.
11. ibid, p.22
12. ibid, p.23
13. ibid, p.29
14. ibid, p.48/9
1. ibid, p.56
2. ibid, p.58
3. ibid, p.123
4. ibid, p.132
5. ibid, p.154

6. ibid, p.164
7. ibid, p.165
8. ibid, p.166
9. ibid, p.194
10. ibid, p.201
11. ibid, 212
12. ibid, p.215
13. ibid, p.232
14. ibid, p.245
15. ibid, p.247
16. ibid, p.251
17. ibid, p.257
18. ibid, p.261
19. ibid, p.271
20. ibid, p.276
21. ibid, p.281
22. ibid, p.288
23. ibid, p.289
24. ibid, p.317
25. ibid, p.329
26. ibid, p.332
27. ibid, p.335
28. Berger Dorothy, *Jean Paul Friedrich Richter* (New York: Twayne Publishers, 1972), p.25
29. Hoffmann, E.T.A, *The Life and Opinions of the Tom Cat Murr* (London: Penguin, 1999), p.xiii
30. Buckminster Lee, p.427
31. ibid, p.429ibid, p.432
32. ibid, p.435
33. ibid, p.441
34. Carlyle, p.27

CHAPTER TWO: THEMES, THEORIES AND THE NOVELS

Many literary critics and historians have stated that the novel began to develop in the eighteenth century, but there were many writers before that time who produced fictional works of a certain length, which were published on broadsheets until chapbooks appeared in the eighteenth century. Pamphlets had been useful for political and religious purposes in the seventeenth century, and the ballad singer-seller also made his commentary in the street, upon events of the time. The small pocket songbook had also been around, extending with it the popular oral tradition of previous centuries.

The Chapbook was a small paper-covered book or pamphlet, usually measuring some three and a half inches by six inches, containing 4, 8, 12, 16, or 24 pages, and always enlivened by the inclusion of crude woodcut illustrations.[1] They were easier to transport, and made available to a wider reading public on the street by salesmen known as chapmen. The biography of Jean Paul by Eliza Buckminster Lee revealed how Jean Paul had made many of his own chapbooks, in which he recorded a great detail of information, and used them for reference in the many learned digressions and extra pages of his novels.

The extent of fictional prose pieces were not uniform in size or appearance either, but works that could be called novels were being written by minor writers for a limited reading audience, through prose pieces such as essays, biographies and drama.

During the early decades of the nineteenth century the reading public began to expand, with new machinery and printing presses, and writers developing new innovative techniques to improve their work and satisfy demand. Those novels dealt with everyday contexts and situations, with subjects such as romance, travel, the historic as well as humour. But the greatest interest of the novel was in its depiction of characters and relationships in a believable story or plot, which made it a precursor to the realist novels of the mid-nineteenth century.

Georg Lukács reinforced that observation when he claimed that, "the novel's manner of portrayal is closer to life, or rather to the normal appearance of life than that of drama…by representing a limited section of reality, it aims to evoke the totality of the process of social development…Society is the principle subject of the novel, that is, man's social life in its ceaseless interaction with surrounding nature, which forms the basis of social activity…"[2] His beliefs revolved around the socialist and historical structures of society, which could be seen in what became known as the realist novels.

A comparison between Realism and Romanticism will provide the information required as to which categorisation Jean Paul can be considered for. To define a particular literary genre is a difficult task, as some characteristics can overlap or works be excluded. However, there are certain characteristics that historically, in their origin and development, are recognised as belonging to particular types of genre. Those forms can also be recognised as ones suited to certain themes and subject matter.

The form of realism had usually been defined as the opposite to Romanticism because it represented everyday realities instead of the inner spiritual and transcendental qualities of the Romantic wanderer. There is an important difference between realism in everyday life and literary realism: the latter has the addition of a fictional plot, whereas in real life something that is real or pertaining to reality is not fiction.

Roland Barthes found realism to be a "literary ideology which corresponds to the 'natural' view [therefore] realist literature tends to conceal the socially relative or constructed nature of language; it helps to confirm the prejudice that there is a form of 'ordinary' language which is somehow natural. This natural language gives us reality 'as it is': it does not –like Romanticism or Symbolism – distort it into subjective shapes, but represents the world to us as God himself might know it."[3]

The period of realism began after the Romantic age, through the mid to late nineteenth century. However, realism had been around as a literary device since the eighteenth century, when the pressures of political, economic and social changes brought with it the advent of a broader novel form. Those social changes of the eighteenth century were different in some respects, having an ideological or political bias, to those arising in the nineteenth century, when the publishing trade was flourishing due to the increased reading population and aftermath of European wars.

During the eighteenth century, realism and classical writings were transmitted through epic poetry, romance, biographies and autobiographies, the Italian novella, moral essays and certain drama productions, but were lagging behind with novel production.

According to Black and Porter, "a long-lasting debate on the rise of the novel has not produced any widespread agreement on exactly how, let alone why, the novel proper finally emerged at the start of the eighteenth century. Some propitious circumstances have been isolated, including the growth of urban living, the possibility of greater privacy, afforded by new architectural styles, alleged signs of greater sexual equality and of a new degree of privacy in everyday life, and even what had been seen as an excess of individualism at the political and economic level."[4]

Authors experimented with different ways of approaching realist literature; some relied upon the old classical models, whilst others attempted the Romantic themes. Realism could incorporate humour and wit, a social commentary; questioning attitudes and values, science fiction, or, the investigation of a crime. Characters also had to be seen as developing morally in an ever-changing society.

The narrative style of the novel meant that the writer worked to arouse the emotions of his readers. Love and death, coupled with shock and horror were powerful subjects, which achieved the desired result. The reader did not want his favourite character to suffer, and so reacted emotionally when the writer manipulated that aspect; when the hero was hurt we felt his pain, and the writer had achieved his effect. By indirect means the writer could direct and alert the reader to recognise familiar situations, and also the motivation, greed and immorality of his characters.

To create a realistic novel the writer needed a plot in which the central story had a conflict to resolve, which needed a good knowledge and experience of life, or chronology, in which the action takes place. He also needed to consider the conclusion, whether through surprise endings or complications of surprise which could produce opposite emotions.

Human interest appeal was the greatest challenge. The author had to create characters who were real, having defined characteristics, ambitions and motives, with personalities that provided a psychological realism The atmosphere, or mood of the novel could differ greatly, from dark, brooding and tragic, making the reader feel the chill and the fear, to scenes of comic effect, although the literary perspective was always controlled by the author through a subjective or objective stance.

Defoe (1661-1731), was the earliest, and greatest, realist writer of his time, the features of which could be recognised in his novels *Robinson Crusoe (1719)* and *Moll Flanders* (1722). Authors such as Richardson, Fielding and Sterne, Jane Austen, William Godwin and Thomas De Quincy were English realist writers, who created characters and dialogue familiar to their readers, giving an overview of the time, but with the more serious questioning of morals, justice and social conditions. Although we recognise such traits in the works of Jean Paul, it is also clear that at times his novels distance themselves from reality.

All authors were writing about the society they were familiar with, reflecting upon and representing that society, and the type of characters they would encounter on a daily basis. They would have been classed as realists rather than Romantics, their philosophy of probability and truth being the most important concern.

As a narrative method, realism gave the novels credibility, honesty, and a true, if at times critical, picture of society. These were some of the necessary features and functions of the realist novel. The most widely read themes of literature in the late eighteenth and early nineteenth centuries were the Romantic and the Gothic. Alongside these, the historical novel could be found, as well as the continuing tradition of humour and satire.

In German literature the novel came in many forms, and the Novelle (*die Novelle*), came to be recognised as an alternative novel form, but with the novel having much more freedom of movement. Chris Baldick defined the Novelle as "a German term for a fictional prose tale that concentrates on a single event or situation, usually with a surprising conclusion."[5] The term was adopted from the Italian, *novella*. The term was introduced into Germany by Goethe, but included works by Tieck, Kleist and Thomas Mann. Bennett distinguished the novella from the short story, which he claimed "was a more modern development, [also, that] the Novelle had a special kind of prose narrative."[6]

He identified Gottfried Keller as one of the more prominent writers who produced Novellen. Interestingly, Blackall stated that in a Novellen, the teller of the story often appeared as a definite character within the narrative, such as could be found in the works of Jean Paul, where, "he himself is always present, either as the master puppeteer, the sovereign god controlling his creations, or even directly as one of the narrators, sometimes with the help of his wife or sister, or as an actual character in the action."[7]

Bennett explained that in the Novelle the action revolved around a striking, fateful event, which befell a certain person or group of persons: an event which was often of supreme importance in the life of the person concerned [and] of the changes which it produced in his life."[8] He illustrated the point by referring to "Kleist's Novelle, *Michael Kohlhaas*, whose horses were taken from him and justice refused him. Out of that event which befell him, was developed the whole action of the Novelle."[9] The illustration highlighted how in the Novelle the passive hero was at the mercy of circumstances which would shape his future fate. Bennett described it as "presentation, not of character as fate, as in the drama, but of chance as fate."[10]

Apart from the tensions of the narrative, Bennett stated that the Novelle could produce a happy or tragic ending. It could also present life as fatalistic, but the one particular aspect of the Novelle was its concentration upon the one individual around whom everything else revolved.

Bennett distinguished Friedrich Schlegel as being the first theoretical writer on the Novelle in German literature, and who described it as "an anecdote, a hitherto unknown story, which must be able to arouse interest by itself, without reference to the ordinary course of human culture and history."[11] He pointed out "the possibility of retelling and remodelling already known stories in such a way that they acquire the charm of novelty; and hints here the personality of the narrator may be the real attraction."[12] Bennett pointed out that it was, in that way, characteristic of the Romantic exploitation of the subjective, and that the Novelle provided a subjective outlet, as the narrator gave the objective details, he could also express his own subjective feelings. Bennett again referred to Kleist and "his desperate uncertainty and questioning attitude to life."[13].

Goethe had attempted to define the Novelle, stating that it was "an event which is unheard of, but has taken place."[14] Bennett suggested that it was a 'real' definition, and that "many German works were labelled as being Novelle, but were actually not."[15] He cited Wieland's definition that the events of the novella should take place in the real world, with Schleiermacher agreeing with him. It confirmed that the fantastic did not then have a place in the Novelle, but as Bennett pointed out "the Romantics did not always accept that definition, but passed between reality and fantasy."[16]

Paul Ernst, who had written extensively about the Novelle form, claimed, "The improbable, that may even be intensified to the impossible, is the very atmosphere in which the Novelle, that sister of the fairy tale, is most at home. It is perhaps the greatest pleasure for the poet, as far as this type of composition is concerned, to represent the improbable in such a manner as to give the impression of the purest probability."[17]

Ludwig Tieck also contributed to the debate about the definition of the Novelle. In 1829 he stated in his collected works that "the Novelle presents in a clear line a happening of greater or less importance, which, however easily it may occur, is yet strange, and perhaps unique. This twist in the story, this point from which it takes unexpectedly a completely different direction, and develops consequences which are nevertheless natural and in keeping with character and circumstances, will impress itself the more firmly upon the imagination of the reader, in so far as the story in spite of its strangeness might under other circumstances be completely commonplace." He continued, "A genuine Novelle may be bizarre, arbitrary, fantastic, witty, garrulous, losing itself completely even in the presentation of side issues, tragic as well as comic, profound and saucy- all of these qualities are possible in the Novelle- but it will always have that extraordinary and striking turning-point which distinguishes it from every other narrative form."[18] Tieck gave a comprehensive account of the Novelle, in which the turning point, that part of the action which takes an unexpected turn, is central to the genre.

Paul Heyse, was according to Bennett the most famous theorist, and who, in 1871 declared that the Novelle should "present to us a significant human fate, an emotional, intellectual or moral conflict, and that it should reveal to us by means of an unusual happening a new aspect of human nature…within a restricted framework… impress themselves profoundly upon the memory."[19] As Bennett implied the theory of Heyse was not very "profound nor very illuminating,"[20] and concluded that the Novelle must have a definite subject matter and make an impression on the memory.

Bennett's assessment of the various theories led him to conclude that the Novelle must contain events rather than actions, "with one single event that had an effect upon the person or persons, characters who are fully formed, chance that is presented as fate, some aspect of life which arouses interest –strangeness or remoteness, action taking place in a world of reality and not imagination, its origin and home being in a cultured society, and the turning point of the narrative with a satisfactory conclusion."[21]

Throughout Europe during the eighteenth century, particularly after the French Revolution and into the early nineteenth century, writers began to concentrate upon human aspects in their works; emotions, thoughts, imagination and the total freedom of expression, encouraging a type of universal humanity. All previous rigid and classical structures were abandoned in favour of a liberal 'human' and 'naturist' approach that became known as the Romantic Movement. Throughout Europe each country had their own interpretations of Romanticism, whether adopting a forward-looking approach or looking back to the past for answers.

Romantic poets offered a new perspective of Romantic thought, and yet all dealt with the underlying theme of time, the universe, God and the consciousness of the individual and his destiny. The concerns of the nation were voiced not just in poetry, but in prefaces, theoretical texts and manifestos during the late eighteenth century through to the first decades of the nineteenth century. Their influence developed as a reaction, not just to the French Revolution and European wars, but also to the Industrial Revolution taking place in England. The English Romantic poets, in similar vein to the Germans, sought to express their feelings about and within the natural world, recording life as they perceived it.

Prior to the eighteenth century artists of all genres of art relied upon Greek and Roman traditions when it came to form. Traditional classicism meant that artists all followed the same rigid constraints of style. During the eighteenth century changes in literary style began to evolve and the dawn of what became known as the Enlightenment, brought a new appreciation of the aesthetic. Romanticism removed all former constraints and allowed artists to follow their own individual form of expression within its intellectual and cultural aspects.

Romanticism, in its broadest sense, was a search for truth. It was a movement, a reaction to the past, to oppressions and wars, confinements and prejudice, allowing the individual to become aware of himself and his own mortality, to make his own choices, and most of all to give free reign to the emotions. It was after all an opposing product of previous social and cultural revolutions. In such a sense it could be argued that Romanticism was that which happened at a certain time in history, in a certain place and to certain individuals. It was, in that respect, limited time-wise, Authors and critics have sought to define the term 'Romanticism,' over the years and have offered many alternatives. Lilian Furst[22] listed a host of definitions that had been put forward over the years, whilst Arthur O Lovejoy pointed out that "Romanticism offers one of the most complicated, fascinating, and instructive of all problems in semantics."[23]

It was often said that Romanticism was the opposite of Realism, but taking into account that the individual faces the full forces of nature and questions man's place in the great scheme of things, then Romanticism could also be very 'real.' Life and death are, after all, very human and very real. Mark Kipperman stated that "the most Romantic poems begin with something very wrong," and that the poet had to "define his own predicament…overcoming his deepest anxiety…his weapons are few…and his magic is his faith in the human imagination."[24]

Romanticism could also be described as a 'function', rather than having a particular dictionary definition, with its most outstanding function being freedom of expression; writers and poets could question and display their thoughts and emotions through their works. The overall function of Romanticism that writers and poets agreed upon seemed to be the quest to find man's place in society and the universe.

Background was another important element for such examination, the backdrop of which was the full force of nature, whether in her bitter coldness, stormy and tempestuous rages, or in the full bloom of a summer's day. Nature and man were, in such an instance, as one. However, because this image of Romanticism appeared to be the capture of a moment in time, it would be a false image.

Romanticism was very multifaceted, containing emotions, particularly love and passion, "the Romanticists' thoughts and feelings focussed upon love; their most profound experience was that of love…Irrational and transcendental powers, the heart and the spirit, the poetic and the philosophic, enabled each individual, isolated, uncertain, anxious, to realize oneness with the group."[25] Other elements were travel and wanderings, mysterious events, and the heroic, coupled with the contrast of man-made and natural justice; a complete life-death scenario.

Examples of such could be seen in the poems of Ossian, (although there were many fabrications and translations of the poems) translated by James Macpherson, with their dramatic Northern backdrop, which had proved a huge success with readers across Europe and in Germany. The appeal of the poems lay in their primitivism and qualities of the sublime, "grand, pathetic, serious, grave, wild and Romantic, sublime and tender,"[26] were some of the epithets used to describe Ossian's 'Fingal.'

The myths also later influenced the works of German Romantics Goethe, Herder and Schiller. Despite being fictitious, they illustrated universal truths. The mystery of nature, a subject close to the heart of Romanticism had always been explored through mythology, explained as the will and action of the gods in classical literatures. The forces of nature were symbolized by gods of the sky, land and sea, embracing the nature spirits of the forests, fields and rivers, who could create a storm or bring calm in vivid and powerful lyrical descriptions.

Germany had become the main vehicle for transporting what became known as, the Romantic Movement. The Romantic School, as it became known, with its founders; the Schlegel brothers, Tieck, Novalis, Fichte and others, adopted the mantle, which soon spread, and became recognised across Europe.

In England there was an enthusiastic welcome for all things associated with Romanticism. The German writers were given a glowing reference by Thomas Carlyle, who admired the works of Goethe, Schiller and Jean Paul Richter. England adopted Romanticism very early in the nineteenth century prior to the Victorian Age, as the works of the German writers began to pour into the country. Although there were differences and similarities with each country, the German Romantics had a strong regard for the English interpretation, and importance that they too placed upon the imagination.

The Romantic Movement was built upon the theory of imagination as artists turned their backs on religious, intellectual and political ideologies in favour of all things mystical, spiritual and earthly in all artistic endeavours. Its main focus was on the inner mind of the individual as well as an appreciation of the beauty of nature, the aesthetic and sublime through a very individual and personalised vision of the world.

The themes of Romanticism were very popular with the reading public who could relate it to themselves, their own reality and consciousness. It eventually became an international movement, reaching from Europe to America and Russia.

Many influential figures were involved in the development of the concept known as Romanticism, such as Rousseau, Kant and Herder, who sought a new national identity for the fragmented Germany following on from the *Sturm and Drang* of the 1770's.

Isaiah Berlin attempted to catch the essence of the Romantic movement, and stated, "whether by external inspection, the most subtle insight so long as they labour under the illusion that it is possible, once and for all to write down, to describe, to give any finality to the process which they are trying to nail down, unreality and fantasy will result – an attempt, always to cage the uncageable, to pursue truth where there is no truth, to stop the unceasing flow, to catch movement by means of rest, to catch time by means of space, to catch light by means of darkness. That is the Romantic sermon."[27] The statement was illuminating, and unlike many other opinions about it, Berlin noted not just the revolutionary aspects, but also what can be the contradictory nature of Romanticism.

Berlin also noted the widespread adoption of Romanticism in other countries where there was" some kind of social discontent and dissatisfaction, particularly to countries oppressed…perhaps it found its most passionate expression in England, where Byron was the leader of the entire Romantic Movement, in the sense that Byronism became almost synonymous with Romanticism in the early nineteenth century." He continued, the French Romantics from Hugo onwards are disciples of Byron. Byron and Goethe saw the movement rushing head-on over all obstacles…the waters of the Rhine rise and cover this violent, this chaotic, this unstoppable, this incurable disease by which all mortals are affected. That is the heart of the Romantic Movement in Europe."[28]

An imaginative and extreme form of Romanticism, characteristic of the period, was the Gothic. It brought with it fear and terror from the darkest depths of humanity. The popularity of Gothic fiction had been a literary phenomena of the mid-eighteenth and early nineteenth centuries.

The darker side of Romanticism became known as the Gothic element. Dark, over-imaginative with excessive uses of terror and fear; ghosts and supernatural wanderings, medieval castles, churches and graveyards to landscapes and wild, mountainous terrains, and death -the Gothic fiction of imagination and heightened emotional states contained them all, and was very popular with the reading public of the eighteenth and early nineteenth centuries.

Fred Botting provided a condensed historical background to the rise of the Gothic novel, stating that "historically the Gothic was associated with the northern Germanic nations whose "fierce avowal of the values of freedom and democracy was claimed as an ancient heritage. Opposed to all forms of tyranny and slavery, the warlike, Gothic tribes of northern Europe were popularly believed to have brought down the Roman Empire. Roman tyranny was subsequently identified with the Catholic Church, and the production of Gothic novels in northern European Protestant countries often had an anti-Catholic subtext."[29]

The major Gothic issues were itemised according to Rictor Norton as being, "the aesthetics of the Sublime, religion and the supernatural, the influence of the ancient romance, the discourse of Enlightenment reason versus Romantic imagination – the hobgoblin machinery of vampires, spectres, orphans, the Inquisition, nuns, storm and ruined castles, labyrinths and mystic forests, alongside social themes of prison reform, revolutionary politics, mother-daughter relationships, illicit sexuality, sensibility and madness."[30]

Fred Botting added to the complexities of the Gothic novel commenting that "uncertainties about the nature of power, law, society, family and sexuality dominate Gothic fiction. They are linked to wider threats of disintegration manifested most forcefully in political revolution," and pointed out that "the decade of the French Revolution was also the period when the Gothic novel was at its most popular."[31]

Supernatural and terrifying legends have been passed down through endless generations, with elaborations from each, from word of mouth (oral tradition) to literary forms. Within the onset of the Romantic Movement, the Gothic once again appeared in poetic and narrative, architectural, dramatic and artistic form.

Apparitions and visions appeared as constant members of the Gothic novel, whether to warn or accuse, they always had the capability to terrify. Daniel Defoe composed an *Essay on the History and Reality of Apparitions*, in which he wrote about various instances of haunting, visions, spiritual and ghostly apparitions. His rational enquiry about the spirit world led him firstly to question what a spirit or ghost actually was. In his discussion about spirits he declared that "the inhabitants which I suggest are created for the invisible world, are spirits, invisible substances, bodies without body, such as are proper for the expanse in which they live, and eligible for us to conceive of; and though we cannot grasp a spirit with our hands, feel it and see it, yet we can in some manner conceive of it [but] cannot account for them to ourselves or anyone else [or say] anything that is probable or rational."[32]

Defoe's belief appeared to be that the few true sightings or involvement of spirit may have been "of those blessed angelic spirits, who may so far have concerned themselves in some cases of violence, oppression, manifest and atrocious frauds, to alarm the offenders, and thereby bring them to do right, as well for their own good as for the relief of the oppressed sufferers, who, perhaps, have invoked the Divine justice against them."[33]

He explained that "conscience, indeed, is a frightful apparition itself, and I make no question but it oftentimes haunts an oppressing criminal into restitution, and is a ghost to him sleeping or waking." He continued, "Conscience makes ghosts walk and departed souls appear."[34]

Defoe used the image of murder, claiming that the soul of the murderer was like the ocean in a tempest, he was in continual motion, restless and raging; and the guilt of the fact, like the winds to the sea, laid on his mind as a constant pressure, and adds to that (still like the seas); it is hurried about by its own weight, rolling to and again, motion increasing motion, till it becomes a mere mass of horror and confusion."[35]

Although Defoe appears to have concluded that man was his own judge and his conscience his jury, in the following chapter he returned to the argument that spirits do exist and that cannot be refuted, as if, "arguing that the existence of the sun when it is clouded and eclipsed."[36] He went on to claim that "history, experience and report of all ages confirm it [and that] history is full of examples."[37] His essay was full of stories that had been told to him or by manuscripts of experiences passed down to him that demonstrated and so proved the issue of visions, appearances, and uncanny events.

During the eighteenth century the Church, which had always been the centre of people's lives and livelihood, found itself under attack alongside that of its political rulers. The French Revolution was the catalyst for the crisis, and collapse of the old ways of the Church where the clergy had been a privileged class. According to Alec Vidler, "It was said that they [the clergy] administered more provinces than sacraments!"[38] The central figures, bishops and higher clergy lived as aristocrats, whilst the poorer country priests had to rely upon the collection of taxes from the farmers and land-workers.

The eventual reform, the Civil Constitution of the Clergy, was based upon elections, but still remained a domain for the aristocracy. The poorer curates who refused to align themselves with the new constitution, found their lives at risk when they were then exposed as revolutionaries. Napoleon's arrival meant that a form of social unity brought together the warring factions in Church divisions, and included approval from the Pope, who had had only been formerly recognised as an invisible figure-head. It was a ploy that was successful as the clergy would, after an initial payment from the state, then have to look to the Pope for further funding.

Napoleon's self-destructive concordat giving him supreme control of the Church in France, was very unpopular with the Pope, who did not agree with the new measures insisted upon by Napoleon. The result added to the downfall of Napoleon, leaving the Church in a state of limbo. The positive elements to emerge from all the upheavals were a sense of freedom and equality, issues that had been at the heart of the troubles.

At the same time, in Germany, Kant, Hegel and their followers were developing their own philosophies about religion, reason, freedom and immortality, having differing theories when it came to the subject of God and Christianity. Frederick Schlegel attempted to create a new religion, proposing that "a new religion that would absorb the French Revolution as Christianity had absorbed the Roman Empire."[39] His ideas won some following, and Germany began to revive the Catholic theology, spurred on by the emergence of Romanticism. Vidler stated that "they contrasted the universality of the Catholic Church with the nationalism and territorialism with which Protestantism was compounded, [and continued that] they had staked out a claim for the ideas that reason and revelation, nature and supernature, liberty and authority, are not opposed to one another but are complimentary, and that

Catholicism is capable of meeting not only Protestantism but historical criticism, science, and philosophy in an open encounter."[40]

In England, the influences from both Germany and France were being felt, although the Church of England had held on to its position of power for centuries, its belief was "that religion, as taught in the Church of England meant moral obedience to the will of God."[41] People had always conditionally accepted the doctrine without question. Priests and all clergy were treated as respected members of society, even though they had clung on to the privileges and riches their situation brought them. On the positive side, with backing from the government the Church built schools to promote education, and new churches with accommodation for its clergy. Whether their educational doctrines were appreciated was a matter for conjecture. The emphasis was firmly on rote learning, with a good helping of hell and damnation thrown in for good measure.

During the century of discontent, writers could not help but vent their feelings about the clergy, and the corruptness and abuses of the Church in their works, from Sterne's *Tristram Shandy*, and Matthew Lewis's *The Monk*, in England, to Manzoni's *I promess sposi*, in Italy. The Marquis De Sade's *Justine*, Chateaubriand, Balzac and Diderot's *Jacques the Fatalist* and *The Nun*, in France raised questions about Christianity, whilst in Russia there was a condemnation by Catherine II for any writer attacking the aristocracy, such as Alexander Radishchev who was exiled for writing his book *Journey from St. Petersburg to Moscow*, which condemned autocracy and serfdom.

In Germany, Pietism, a personal form of worship for people who had like-minded beliefs, and who believed that the church was out of date and also corrupt was being practised. Its members were seen as rebels who were in opposition to church discipline and authority. It was explained by Black and Porter as,

"Pietism, a sector of Protestantism, in which the conscience of the individual [is] in strict adherence to Biblical precept forms the basis of faith and conduct. The practice of self-examination encouraged by this attitude promoted a form of expression which influenced literary production most effectively at a time when the Enlightenment was on the wane. Many great writers of the time, such as Lessing, Klopstock, Goethe, Schiller, Holderlin and Novalis were affected in one form or another by Pietism and gave expression to its tenets."[42]

Kleist, in contrast, questioned the rituals of the Catholic Church in his novel *The Marquis of O-* whether divine intervention or actual magic was used, and if we should embrace, or fear the Church. Although the Catholic cities were not affected by literary output as in the Protestant parts of Germany, and the "division between the two forms of the Christian religion determined the course of literary developments more markedly in Germany than elsewhere in Europe."[43] But it is in the novels of Jean Paul that Christian beliefs were put to the test, through dual personalities, and visions, secret sects, the desire to see the next world and, the need to see and recognise, God. The immortality of the soul had almost become an obsession within his works, which celebrated the union of man within nature.

Another genre of the novel was the humorous, bawdy or witty satire. Jean Paul Richter commented that "the comic cannot exist without sensuousness; the comic writer fastens our mind upon physical detail."[44] Like all writers of humour, Jean Paul needed characters in all their guises for the study of human behaviour, habits, and environments in his novels, those being the essential tools of the comic, artist and writer of wit.

Humour is a part of the human character, an opposite of sadness. There are different types and forms of humour; satire, irony, comic and others, with different applications and techniques for individual situations. William Hazlitt pointed out that "we laugh at a thing merely because we ought not, [and that] you cannot force people to laugh, you cannot give a reason why they should laugh; they must laugh at themselves or not at all."[45]

Wit, or *witz*, was an important part of Germany's literary and cultural history, and was an important element in the novels of Jean Paul Richter. Many fiction writers in the seventeenth century had regarded humour as being an important part of their everyday observations for the contexts of their novels.

Carl Hill discussed the journey of wit in his book *The Soul of Wit*, which also had reference to the opinions of Jean Paul. With its emphasis on Germany, Hill discussed the authors and philosophers who have written with, and about, the concept we know as wit, starting with a humorous line of "in the beginning there was God, and God was witty."[46] He followed that with various quotes from early authors such as Georg Nigrinus that "the female sex is…improvident, because it does not observe all that it sees and hears with wit and reason." Hill gave the witty translation of the quote as being; "And so God saw that He must give man a companion and thus created woman. But this was no big help."[47] Although the comments sounded cruel, the reader could not help but smile, and that was the successful aim of wit.

Wit had always been a difficult term to define accurately and was used in various forms, even by the English, who appeared to have a better idea of its use, having had a better sense of humour than the Germans, who looked to, and emulated the French, where it was employed by the aristocracy. Hill pointed out that "Ariste and Eugene [were] at pains to point out that it is not really the Germans' fault if they're a little dim – it is just that they live in a cold climate and tend to be fat, factors which naturally slow one's intellectual development."[48] Wit was, in that respect seen as a rich man's domain, until later years when writers incorporated it into their novels.

The only problem was that in the beginning, it was only people who had money who could afford to purchase the works.

From the later seventeenth century through to the early nineteenth century satire became a popular form of literary device employed by, and used in various different ways by writers such as Dryden, Pope, Swift, Johnson and Defoe, followed by Goldsmith, Peacock, Smollett and Sterne, Austen, and many others up to Lord Byron in the nineteenth century. Satire as a literary technique had been used for centuries, the Classical writer Juvenal (55-130 AD) had written satire influencing "lots of English writers who later wrote raunchy and /or satirical stuff, including Chaucer, Donne, Swift, Pope and Dr Johnson."[49]

The meaning of wit had gradually begun to change, and was used by the common man, who viewed it with humour and laughter as it aimed its target at society, individual errors and caricature of individuals. Hill referred to Börne's comments about Goethe and Schiller, "our two greatest poets were so completely lacking in Witz; but I thought, they have nobility of spirit and are reluctant in their public appearances to show any familiarity...at home when no one is around they are probably very witty. But when I read their correspondence, I found that in their nightgowns they have no more Witz than they would a dagger at their side."[50]

Hodgart gave the original definition for the term satire (from *Webster's New World Dictionary*), in literature as being "in which vice, follies, stupidities and abuses, etc., are held up to ridicule and contempt."[51] He went on to discuss the possible origins of satire in its various forms, including the oral tradition, as opposed to the written, in which a person could defend himself by using cutting, witty remarks. This clever technique implied also, that wit can be measured, being of use in different ways for different situations; in anger to humiliate, or "to look on the world with gentle irony."[52] Arthur Pollard pointed out that the job of the satirist was, "to persuade and convince," and that we should recognise the satirist as "an artist and satire as an art."[53]

The aim of satire was to make us look at the situation or individuals with a common sense, down-to-earth approach that reduced everything to the plain and simple. By doing so, however, the author had expected the reader to understand when something or someone was being the subject of irony and satire. The techniques involved were by direct means; insult and shock effect, or by more subtle methods of irony and double meanings. Exaggeration was another technique that would be employed, although it was only required when a more 'comic' effect was needed. By reducing his situations to a logical extreme the writer could also expose the irresponsible or foolhardy ideas and actions of his characters.

There are many additional devices used by the writer of satire, such as irony, where there is a discrepancy between what a person says and what he does, and is more of an indirect form, or the invective, a bitter satire, which, as a tool of anger, can be used in extreme moments of anger. The difference between humour and satire is that we can laugh at ourselves as a group, in a familiar situation, but satire is when something is brought to our notice in a certain situation or by an individual, where that activity or belief will be questioned, and suggestions offered to rectify or morally correct that behaviour, or, as Pollard pointed out, "satire is always acutely conscious of the difference between what things are and what they ought to be."[54]

In most cases the writer will urge us to smile at the offender, and become involved in the joke, with the understanding, tolerance and recognition of human nature. Swift observed that "satire is a sort of glass, wherein beholders do generally discover everybody's face but their own, which is the chief reason for that kind of reception it meets in the world and that so very few are offended with it."[55] The writer of satire has to walk a fine line and avoid preaching or moralising, which can become boring and monotonous for the reader, whilst also losing the humour and warmth of the plot. He has to remain detached and give a variety of wit and satire, alongside a clever choice of words and emotions, in order to keep the reader interested and laughing in a constructive way, and so offers a link between society and the individual.

Theorists have stated that there are different types of humour, and that writers used different forms and techniques when applying it. For that reason, and because some of our own English writers also applied the technique during the eighteenth and nineteenth centuries, satire as a cultural and literary device, could not be ignored.

Robert M. Wernaer in his article *Romanticism and the German Romantic School*, quoted Friedrich Schlegel, who claimed "if one desired to be flippant over a matter that really deserves profound attention and respect, one might suggest that the Romanticists, having invented a universe drowned in a sea of emotion, suddenly discovered that to be complete the world should have wit as well, and so they discovered irony as a sort of little island where they might take refuge from time to time to laugh at themselves and the world they had made."[56] The comments shed light upon the important aspect of humour, which was adopted and used in creative and original ways by the writers of the late eighteenth and early nineteenth centuries, Pope, Sterne and particularly Jean Paul Richter, all used aspects of humour, either to laugh at their characters, their situations, or by adding witty remarks in digressions which would make readers smile.
of their own streets."[57]

But it was the love of his homeland which inspired Jean Paul to paint a glorious picture of German scenery. The sentiments and positive comments about the landscapes of Germany were echoed by many writers, but not more so than Jean Paul Richter, whose love for his country and his own personal surroundings surfaced in all his works. His settings were powerful descriptions of nature, the plants, flowers, mountains, and hills, that "sounded like a lovely echo from ancient time," with various colours and changes of the sky affecting the moods of a scene, as "stars peered out in the twilight, and lent wings to their souls."[58]

Herder, who was a friend of Jean Paul's, and considered one of the leading figures of the Romantic Movement, concluded and echoed the sentiments of his friend in a letter to his future wife, Caroline Flachsland, that the countryside of Germany was "the most beautiful, the most rugged, the most German, the most Romantic region of the world. The very same field on which Hermann fought and Varus was defeated; still an awful, rugged, Romantic valley surrounded by singular mountains." Herder continued to link the national character of the Germans with his observations, claiming, "However much of the German valour and of the Klopstockian ideal of morality and greatness may be lost, the soul is nevertheless disposed by the daring, singular demeanour of this Germany to believe that there is a beautiful, rugged German nature."[59]

As well as being treated to the panoramic vistas of German landscapes in the works of Jean Paul, music was also a great part of German culture. Dorothy Berger commented upon the musical aspects in the novels of Jean Paul, and that he had said, in his *Comic Appendix* to *Titan*, in his defence of the novel, and with reference to Mozart's *Magic Flute*, "the audience has to enjoy the "chaos of all the instruments, all the actors, their visual pantomime and exotic sound effects… which was more demanding than the reading of the novel."[60]

But, asked Dorothy Berger, "where was the good music in the novel?"[61] Music played an important role in Jean Paul's novels, always present, even when not being directly alluded to. The sounds of nature were forever present, and emitted their own kinds of music in the background, dictating the pace and tension of many of the scenes. We listened to church bells ringing, flutes playing, the Aeolian harp, and harmonica-tones, even the sound of the clock striking the hour resounded loudly through the narrative.

Mason stated that "if Schumann is incomparable in his insight into the storm and stress of the human heart, Mendelssohn is one of the great landscape painters."[62] Unlike the freedom and imagination of expression, displayed by other musicians, however, Mendelssohn "was never engaged with his own emotions, but played like a disembodied spirit about the impressions he was imagining…he is always behind his work rather than in it."[63]

His Italian Symphony, however, has "flutes and clarinets and violins in their upper register, and trumpets playing piano [sounding] not like mere orchestral instruments, but angelic voices in a remote sky…few composers have so fully realized how little an effect is due to the mere quantity of the sounds, how much to their skilful composition."[64] Mason concluded that "as long as Mendelssohn maintained his instinctive aloofness from human emotion, so long as, dwelling in his heaven of imagination, he painted delicate aquarelles of fairyland and Romantic natural scenery, he was an incomparable master."[65]

Schiller, as writer, poet and dramatist, commented about the power of the various art forms, "poetry when most fully developed, must grip us as powerfully as music does," whilst Ernst Hoffmann, discussing the music of Beethoven, said, "it sets in motion the lever of fear, of awe, of horror, of suffering, and awakens that infinite longing which is the essence of Romanticism."[65]

The decade 1790-1800 had been influential not just in a political or historical sense, but in music, also. It not only laid the foundations of Romantic opera but created a whole new musical form in Germany, France and in some parts of Italy. Abrahams stated that as Haydn had dominated the 1790's Beethoven (1770-1827), was already busily working on his *Eroica Symphony.* He claimed, however, that there "was nothing Romantic in the music of the French Revolution, nor anything nationalistic or even revolutionary," but that in Beethoven "there were plenty of premonitions of Romanticism but not in its full ripening…the Romantic instrumental composers were more and more concerned with the expression of defined emotions even pictorial or literary images…Beethoven had become more and more an isolated figure, immensely respected but detached in spirit from the music scene rather than at its centre."[66]

Abrahams noted how one important symptom of Romanticism 'the consciousness of nationality' which was particularly strong in Germany, where a "sense of German nationhood, of a common fatherland, had previously been stifled," and he described briefly, the state of affairs in Germany; of how, when Napoleon had moved into Germany he had been welcomed by some and hated by others. Goethe had been impressed by him, commenting, "The hero grows in stature as more is known about him." Beethoven, it was claimed stated that "at one time I couldn't bear him, now I think quite differently."[67]

Referring to the Age of Beethoven as an age in transition, Abrahams, took an overall view of Europe at that time, of how opera in Italy had continued to flourish, whilst in England, after Haydn's visits during the 1790's, the Philharmonic Society emerged and the instruments; guitar, flute, harp, and pianoforte began to rise in popularity.

In France, music had become an outlet for all the emotions, with the aftermath of the revolution which led to a saturation of musical festivals in the heart of Paris, which were always concluded with cannon fire. The practice spread into the concert halls, where it did not go unnoticed that it was a reminder of the storming of the Bastille. The French continued to celebrate music, people and events in remembrance of the revolution. Russia had adopted the Italian opera under the Empress, Catherine the Great, despite being tone-deaf. The Italian opera and its musical influences pervaded much of Europe, whose own musicians had to battle with it in order to be heard, and to bring the importance of their own national music back to the fore. The opera had, however, always been a suitable genre in which to articulate social conditions.

It was not until he was nearly thirty years old that Beethoven appeared before the public with his *First Symphony*. Spending most of his life in Vienna, Beethoven "wrote nine symphonies, seven concerts, sixteen string quartets, and thirty-two piano sonatas, as well as other orchestral, chamber and keyboard works."[68]

In a chapter on the construction of Beethoven, Knittel cited the contents of a lady from a young lady, Bettina Brentano von Arnim, to Goethe. She claimed, "When I saw him of whom I shall now speak to you, I forgot the whole world," and further, "I may confess I believe in a divine magic which is the essence of intellectual life…all human activities toss around him like mechanism." Beethoven had replied to her,

"Music is the mediator between the life of the mind and the senses."[69] Knittel claimed that there had been some cast over the supposed correspondence between Bettina and Beethoven, whilst Romain Rolland praised her deep insight into the world of Goethe, and that, "none whose influence upon Goethe was more durable, and none, perhaps, who understood the poet better than Bettina von Arnim Brentano, the writer, musician, and champion of political freedom, the great dreamer and great lover, [and that] "if Bettina had a deep insight into Goethe's gigantic mind, she had an equally clear understanding of one who was his peer as no other, Beethoven."[70] It was Bettina who brought the two giants, Beethoven and Goethe, together.

Of the senses, Beethoven had lost his hearing, which would have ended the career of any other musician, but not Beethoven. The aesthetical transcendence of his music transported his listeners to a higher plane, with its emotional expressions of pain and suffering, alongside Beethoven's own belief in his abilities and his music; powerful entities that controlled his isolated existence. Those Romantic values culminated in making him the hero of the German nationalism movement, and the patron of musical Romanticism.

Beethoven had told Bettina, "speak to Goethe of me; tell him that he must hear my symphonies! He will agree with me that music is the single, the immaterial entry into a higher world of knowledge which envelopes man but which he cannot understand...what the soul receives from music through the senses is spiritual revelation incarnate...with all my heart I long for him to teach me."[71] Goethe "who was quite at a loss to express his appreciation of music, complimented the musician on his technique and on his clear-cut playing, with the air of one deeply impressed. But the aesthetic, the reasoned judgment which Beethoven looked for from a man like Goethe, was not forthcoming because Goethe had, in fact, none to offer; he did not understand...Beethoven exploded."[72] That episode marked the end of the friendship, although each always had a grudging respect for the other. Beethoven later wrote the music to *Egmont* as well as several poems by Goethe. One of his best known literary settings was the fourth movement of the Ninth Symphony, the text of which consisted of the first five stanzas of Schiller's *An die Freude.*

René Wellek concluded that it was the "German Romantic writers [who] were the contemporaries of the flowering of German music; of Beethoven, Schubert, Schumann, Weber, and others, many of whom used German poetry of the age as texts for their songs, or, like Beethoven, as inspiration for their symphonies… was a significant characteristic of Romanticism, [but] which did not appear as early in England. In not wanting to obscure the movement from its international position, Wellek pointed out that although the impetus may have originated in Germany, the other European countries took the sentiments and developed their own forms of Romanticism."[73]

Thomas De Quincy stated that "before 1789 good authors were rare in Germany," and asked, who is my favourite author?" He gave the answer; both Schiller and Jean Paul. "Schiller," he wrote, "I love his works chiefly because I venerate the memory of the man: whereas, in the case of Richter, my veneration and affection for the man is founded wholly on my knowledge of his works." De Quincy went so far as to claim that Jean Paul was "by far the most eminent artist – since the time of

Shakespeare, and that "it is to the honour of Jean Paul...he constantly reminds me of Shakespeare. Everywhere a spirit of kindness prevails: his satire is everywhere playful, delicate, and clad in smiles, never bitter, scornful or malignant...Jean Paul's works are the galaxy of the German literary firmament."[74]

The novels written by Jean Paul appeared at regular intervals from 1783 until his death in 1825. Prior to his death he had written the novel *Selena,* and was attempting to complete his autobiography, which he had not begun until 1818, according to George Stuart Collins. The autobiography presented Jean Paul as the "Professor of his own life history, and the three chapters he completed [up to 1776] are called Lectures. These three chapters form the first part of the long biography of Jean Paul by Christian Otto and Ernst Förster... the three lectures which we have, caused great regret that Jean Paul could not have completed his autobiography. No doubt, however, the very circumstances which caused him to relinquish the task, unfinished...might have made the remainder of the work a sharp contrast with the portion completed."[75]

Jean Paul's entrance into the world of literature was, initially, through social satire. Many of his works were in some respects biographical, until experience and maturity led him into the more diverse areas of Romanticism, humour and sentiment. His one consistency was in his philosophy of nature and the universe. Stahl concluded that some of the plots invented by Jean Paul in his novels were, "pointlessly bizarre; in fact, the mistaken or masked identities, cryptic events and sensational revelations often have an ulterior significance – they are emblems of psychological states and crises, spiritual deaths, rejuvenations and resurrections. Alongside – and sometimes embedded within – the tangled intrigues of these stories with their sublime or demonic characters are studies of idyllic contentment in cheerful poverty, or portraits of amiable eccentricity."[76]

Stahl's assessment of the novels gave a multifaceted view of the complexity of scene, the psychology of characters and poetic and Romantic plot, which were invented by Jean Paul. Writing between the eighteenth and nineteenth centuries, meant that influences from both centuries would affect or define the work of a novelist, but Jean Paul's totally unique style made him difficult to categorize. His works included aspects from the sentimental in his past, to the subjective and philosophical questions of his day and the ramifications of writing against the tide of Romanticism, with a large dose of humour to complicate the narrative even more.

Webber also claimed that Jean Paul[was] "a writer who resists categorical judgements [and that] if he is under-read today it is probably not least because he is a misfit in any literary history. His writing seems to correspond most readily to the Sentimentalist novels of eighteenth –century English literature, (the works of such as Sterne or Richardson."[77] But he was writing at the turn of the century where Classicism and Romanticism were established movements. He was also caught up in the philosophical arguments of his day, making his work a combination of idealism, realism, romance, with the philosophical and mystical interwoven. The added use of satire and humour were added to the mix, resulting in a unique narrative product, the equal to any great writer of his day. Jean Paul had discussed his use of humour and how he defined it to his friend Johann Abegg in 1798, as "to find reluctantly the ordinary smallness of human nature while one sublimely hovers midway between pain and elevation above such smallness –to express this is called humour, which offers the appearance of the sublime and of the comic next to one another."[78]

In questioning his own existence, Jean Paul observed the ordinary and everyday humanity, with the mixed emotions of humour and the tragic. His works can be divided into early and later works. The early works of his youth, were enthusiastically written, and often from necessity. In the later works we can appreciate the development and maturity of Jean Paul as a writer and novelist. Although it was through financial need that he wrote his first essays and novels, producing coarse and bitter works of satire, he underwent a transformation following the death of his brother and his friend, which saw a change in his attitude and style.

Further political developments in Germany saw Jean Paul, once again, returning to humour and writing for the people. Satire was the device for which Jean Paul was recognised, alongside the English novelist, Laurence Sterne. Both were equally recognised for their use of digression. Jean Paul had made it his mission to become famous for using more digression than anyone else. It appeared that he was in competition with himself, as his novels illustrated, often making the chronology difficult to follow. "Jean Paul had said that his ambition was to do what no author had ever done: to record for posterity every thought that ever came into his head."[79]

Buckminster Lee also noted how Jean Paul had begun to compile a dictionary, which he added to throughout his life, in which he "wrote down synonyms, and all the shades of meaning of which a word was susceptible. For one word he had found more than two hundred."[80] He was noted for his disregard for form, which made the novels difficult to read, despite his efforts to carefully "sketch the outlines of his characters, the principle scenes, thoughts to be worked in [which he called] *Quarry for Hesperus* or *Quarry for Titan*,"[81] but careful attention to the details revealed the warm and witty nature, the joys and the sorrows of Jean Paul.

Dorothea Berger also raised the issue of digressions and added footnotes, and claimed that Jean Paul employed five different kinds of notes; the first whereby he would give detail and information, to highlight his extensive knowledge; the second, giving hints and illusions that could baffle the reader; the third, which was a running commentary about the action; the fourth translating foreign quotations, "which are sometimes humorous or embarrassing because they destroy the mood of climactic or poetic passages," and the final fifth consisting of aphorisms from his own personal collection.[82]

Jean Paul's linguistic gymnastics may have had his readers shaking their heads with confusion, but the devices he employed allowed him not only to present his story but judge it too. Through such internal speculation Jean Paul could openly display his thoughts and feelings to the readers.

Jean Paul, was introduced to the English reading public, first, by De Quincy and then Carlyle in his *Introduction to German Romance*. Eliza Buckminster Lee supported the introduction when she translated Jean Paul's letters and documents, forming the *Life of Jean Paul Friedrich Richter*. The following comment made by Friedrich Theodor Vischer admitted the difficulties imposed upon the reader by Jean Paul's obscure style, and that "to read Jean Paul is work for a horse."[83]

The Greenland Lawsuits or, *Satirical Sketches* (1783), was the first attempt by a youthful Jean Paul to write a full-length book. It contained a "collection of moral, satirical sketches upon life, under the titles of *Literature, Theology, Family Pride* and *Women and Fops*," of which, Buckminster added, that Jean Paul "could have, at this time, know little."[84] Its attacking approach through bitter satire was not entirely successful, in fact, as Paul Fleming referred to a critical response at the time, "for every reasonable person, the reading of this book will from the very first page produce so much disgust that he will be compelled to put it down."[85] It was followed by a second volume, which also did not receive any great reception, although both earned a small reward. Jean Paul's personal reflections and questioning of faith and humanity were the key themes, with the clergy and nobility being the target of his comments.

In a letter to his friend Vogel, Jean Paul stated that his book "had a thousand faults. It [was] over-laden with comparisons, as the *Eulogy of Stupidy* [a previous essay] was with antithesis. I could collect out of it a regiment of six hundred comparisons. I acknowledge that an excess of comparisons is really a fault; but can cold criticism subdue the charm of rich intemperance....a book without beauties is certainly a bad thing, but one without faults is not, therefore, good."[86] Jean Paul asked his friend, Vogel, if he would read and criticise the manuscript of Greenland Lawsuits, adding, "decide further – if the satire is not too bitter – though I believe satire, like beer, derives its value from its bitterness."[87]

With the publication of the first edition, Jean Paul completed the second, and sent a copy again to Vogel, for his comments. Vogel was very honest with Jean Paul and told him that his second part would be "read only by critics, and will not be understood by the rest of the world," and that the German readers, "found them heavy and uninteresting,"[88] and were not at all interested in satire. A third edition was never published, although revised under the different title, *Selections from the Papers of the Devil*. It was the start of Jean Paul's journey into the literary world, and led to him taming the style of his work, which held more appeal for the German readers.

Maria Wutz or *History of the Contented Little Schoolmaster Maria Wutz* (1793) was Jean Paul's first novel, and based on his educational interests and teaching life. It was also a deeply poetical reflection of life, love and death.

When Jean Paul he had completed writing Maria Wuz, he asked his friend Christian Otto to read and criticise it. "Jean Paul had called it his idyll, as it was the first of his compositions to which he lent his own life...the result was a poetical representation."[89] With recollections of his own childhood and images from the village life in which he had grown up, to creating his own library, as Mrs Buckminster Lee had previously discussed, in the *Life of Jean Paul*. Pages and pages of folded paper were used to provide the space for his lists and books. In the novel he recalled listing and studying Schiller's *The Robbers*, Kant's *Critique of Pure Reason* and Cook's *Voyages Round the World*.

The life of Wuz was a story of a life, full of happiness and contentment, without any extremes of passion, just halcyon days of sunshine and memories gleaned from the small pleasures of life, the regular and consistent everyday village and household activities.

The subject of happiness had a controversial and philosophic role in the enlightenment of the eighteenth century, being discussed throughout Europe as an important element of humanity. Attempts were continually made at that time to quantify happiness; in Germany, Kant linked happiness to the political sphere, making it an objective rather than subjective element of his categories, in which he attempted to make sense of the world. In England, Mary Wollstonecraft claimed in *Vindication of the Rights of Man* (1790) that "the happiness of the whole must arise from the constituent parts, or the essence of justice is sacrificed to a supposed grand arrangement...to labour to increase human happiness by extirpating error, is a masculine godlike affection," while in France, Madame du Châlethad had written in her *Discourse sur le Bonheur* (1779), that happiness "required virtue, health and the capacity for pleasure and passion. It also necessitated the difficult task of riding oneself of prejudices and yet remain open to illusion,"[90] recommending study as a source of happiness.

For Jean Paul the last remarks held a lot of truth as reading and study were his daily sources of happiness. His soul was also always open in a direct, honest and humanitarian way to the understanding of his fellow men, as well as the spiritual aspects of life. *Maria Wuz* presented the light and the dark aspects of life, but consistently enforced love and happiness as the only option for survival.

Jean Paul discussed the love affair of Wuz and his impending marriage to Justina, which he completed with a short passage from the poem by Robert Burns, called *A Lover and his Lass,* where "the flow'rs sprang wanton to be prest/The birds sang love on every spray/Till too, too soon, the glowing west/Proclaim'd the speed of winged day."[91] The story was a deeply personal one, as it was about Jean Paul's own childhood and growth, the death of his father and his relationship with his mother, all told in poetical and colourful images in which, "the melodies of the outer world blended with his dreams."[92] His dream device went on to become a staple feature in his future novels. Although the novel was always referred to as an idyll, it combined death within its context, providing the balance with life and nature. Thoughts of death were never very far away from the thoughts of Jean Paul, who frequently reflected upon the transience of life. Jean Paul stated that "it is a mistake, to define the idyll in terms of the pastoral life or the golden age of humanity; rather, it is the epic presentation of perfect happiness within limits."[93]

Far from the bitter satire of the *Greenland Lawsuits*, Jean Paul referred to it as "the bridge over which he passed from the vinegar fabric where he had worked for nineteen years, when he closed the door to satire, and opened it to all that loved, and rejoiced and wept with human nature."[94] Otto's praise for the story led Jean Paul to venture deeper into romance and sentimentality, with the result being his next novel.

The second novel, accompanying Maria Wuz, was *Lorenz Stark*,(1795), developed by JJ Engel, (1741-1802). It was about a clash of personalities in a family, a complicated love affair, and deceptive appearances combined with the morals and manners of the day, leading to an ultimate conclusion of happiness. It contained commentary on the hierarchy of life and the position of women. The central theme was of love, and presented all the elements normally found in the plays of Shakespeare, especially *Much Ado About Nothing*, where many people were involved in behind-the-scenes planning and persuasions of bringing a couple together. The novel contained moments of pure comedy, as the characters frequently ended up with crossed communications.

The Invisible Lodge was Jean Paul's first novel that brought him some success, and money. It was a combination of romance, education and Jean Paul's own life interwoven into the plot, and illustrated Jean Paul's own creative educational beliefs. The title also gave a clue to aspects of the novel in regard to religion, which were to become an ongoing theme in the works of Jean Paul. The purpose of the title did not become apparent until near to the end of the novel, with the meeting of a group of people in the cave where Gustav had been educated, adding an unexpected twist to the novel.

The novel is half story and half biography, as Jean Paul inserted frequent chapters about his own life. A few of the later chapters were also written about him by his sister, when he was ill. His educational philosophy in *The Invisible Lodge*, he claimed, consisted "in not exciting too early the warmth of emotion, but through mathematics and philosophy forming the understanding to self-activity and leading the fancy to wit; thus protecting the pupil from those moral errors, which are the fruit of a too early excited imagination."[95] There is a recognisable influence from Rousseau in the educational manifesto of Jean Paul.

The narrative style of Jean Paul was individual and quite unique to the normal nineteenth century style of other writers. He was a difficult writer to follow, with fantastic images emerging with each and every page. Webber's 'double,' "had no bodily presence in the *Lodge*, but was represented through the portrait of Gustav."[96]

Multiple reflections are an essential part of the narrative, however, as Jean Paul was not only the narrator in the novel, but taking an active role as tutor of Gustav. So it was through his eyes that all perspectives were reflected. Apart from the main characters of Gustav and Beate, the other characters created were based upon people that Jean Paul had known. "Roper and his wife represented the Oerthelshen married pair, Amandus, -his sick and dying friend Adam von Oerthel and Dr. Fenk was a modification of Herman, destitute, however, of the singular beauty of his friend."[97]

Dr Fenk's appearance caused amazement and hilarity, with his "crazy jokes, [which are much too free],"[98] reflecting the comic side of Jean Paul, but which led to the tragedy of the concluding chapter.

The novel revolved around the experiment and results of 'creative' (but isolated), education of Gustavus, being separated from his parents as a baby to be nurtured, protected and educated by the Genius (Jean Paul), in a subterranean cave between the ages of two to ten years of life, in order for him to "save him from being hardened at once to the beauties of Nature and the distortions of humanity."[99] The master-pupil factor was reminiscent of Rousseau's *Emile*, in which he also stressed the importance of teaching in isolation. Jean Paul's philosophy was to nurture the child by relaxing the old rigid laws and censorship, again following the lead of Rousseau, whose comments about the use of 'chains' in society formed part of his educational philosophy. His open and creative plan was for the child to be interested, to want to learn, and to receive praise where it was due, again all following the examples set by Rousseau.

Following those rules, Gustavus learned to hear before seeing, "because hearing attracts children to seeing more strongly that seeing does to hearing...the feeling for painting develops itself...it deserves the earliest unfolding, because it takes away the grating which sunders us from Nature, because it drives the phantasysing soul out again among external things, and because it turns the German eye to the difficult art of apprehending beautiful forms, [and on music, Jean Paul told us], "that it finds already in the youngest hearts (as with the rudest peoples) responsive chords."[100] Other subjects referred to as part of Jean Paul's educational philosophy were the Fatherland, People, Constitution, Laws, French, Rome, Athens and literary history, arithmetic and geometry. Regarding philosophy, he claimed, "it is no bread earning science, but mental bread itself, and a necessary; and one cannot teach either it or love; both, if taught too early unman body and soul."[101]

Music was frequently referred to in *The Invisible Lodge*. Various instruments are catalogued, heard or played by Jean Paul throughout the novel, including the Moravian choral music, flute, piano, trumpet, harp, mountain bugles and fire-drum. There is always music in the atmosphere of the novel that defines its dramatic purpose of creating heightened emotion and intensity. A good example illustrating the importance of music to Jean Paul was with the organ in the church, "I went up to it as to a thirst quenching fountain. And then with its mighty tones I shook the nightly church and the deaf and dumb...I related to them in organ tones what had become a bare narration…between the tones-there streamed forth a humming sound, as if it were pursuing the wings of time – it bore all my memories and hopes, on its waves floated my throbbing heart…As far back as I can remember a continued tremulous tone has always made me sad."[102]

The cave was the physical womb from where Gustavus eventually emerged, being born into a new world that he understood to be heaven, as life and death took on an alternate perspective. The resurrection of Gustavus took place in the Spring, as in Jean Paul's own entrance into the world. The scene, with its cave image, had been regarded as symbolic, and an enactment of Christ's resurrection.

As Gustavus had been a virtual prisoner for eight years, underground in dark conditions, his freedom had brought with it a naivety that made him isolated and vulnerable, open to the dangers as well as the pleasures of the outside world.

The darkness had also been an element in the teaching of Emile, as Rousseau claimed that it was important for a child to get used to the dark, and not to fear it, but also to strengthen the eyes. In the *Invisible Lodge* the strength of Gustav was compared to the weakness of Amandus through their use of the senses.

His ascension into heaven, a reversal of the facts coupled with deception, was in fact a message by Jean Paul about the finding of spiritual happiness on the earth.

The plot, between man and nature was developed further by Jean Paul's device of the doppelganger, in the form of Amandus, who was identical to Gustavus in appearance. He was introduced as having his eye cut and being blinded by the she-oculist. Again, Jean Paul had put an emphasis on the importance of the senses. The eyes and blindness formed part of the narrative in many of his novels, as a device which would lead to an awakening or regaining of either moral or spiritual awareness.

The complications of the plot in *The Invisible Cave*, surrounded the mirror image of its two main characters, who held a deep admiration and friendship for the other. They then fell in love with Beata, the heroine, but it was not until the eleventh section that the narrator allowed Amandus to regain his sight.

Jean Paul commented on the blinding of Amandus, "I wished my wife might from time to time have a slight cut in that region, because it has a very neat effect."[103] His wife was frequently the butt of his humour and witty remarks, reminding us that he was considering divorce at one stage of his married life, because of her jealousies and insecurities, his decisions to travel alone, and the women in his life. However, when he changed from first to third person narrator in the novel, he became "music master, legal adviser and man of the world [admitting] that he fell in love with all his lady pupils, "in short, there is nothing, leaf-buds, blossom-buds, fruits, with which a man does not get entangled who is a teacher of the piano."[104]

The subject of blindness was a theme often employed by writers of the Romantic period. Edward Larrissy stated that "writers in the Romantic era associated blindness with intense inward vision," and that "the blind possessed a compensatory sensitivity to sounds and music, and a concomitant facility at musical performance."[105] He pointed out that blindness was a useful condition for the writer to incorporate into his narrative, whether to prove they are as competent as the seeing person, as in Rousseau's *Emile*, or, to find goodness and purity through their blindness, or, being blind from birth, reflecting attitudes from people around them.[106] Jean Paul's use of blindness highlights philosophical and poetical contexts, which paved the way for greater spiritual insight.

In the *Second Extra Leaf*, Jean Paul made an extensive and inquisitive enquiry into the nature of marriage and divorce. We are aware from his biography by Buckminster- Lee, that the wife of Jean Paul had changed in character from the woman he had married, and that he was considering a divorce. At the conclusion of the extra leaf, he sums up the subject, claiming, "and today is three years since I too was joined in marriage…but the straw-wreath oration on that occasion was too pure to repeat."[107]

Indeed, his appreciation for the female seemed to have taken a tumble, also, as he remarked in the novel, when considering the character of Beata, who had taken, "an active interest in our talk; for he has a notion that one may talk with a woman about heaven and hell, god and the Fatherland, and yet she will be thinking of nothing all the while she listens, but her figure, her attitude, her dress."[108]

On wit, Jean Paul remarked, "Heavens! I shall have had more wit here than one may well give me credit for; but let a live man once try it, and write upon love and refrain from wit! It is almost impracticable…the romancer has therefore an advantage over the biographer (which is I): he keeps close by his hero."[109]

Although he had an abundance of thoughts and ideas, Jean Paul's knowledge of the world and its people were limited. He confessed to his friend Otto, "think of my disadvantageous situation as a romance writer, that I can avail myself of so few living characters, as models, that I have never seen the higher ranks of life, - and be lenient."[110]

But his golden moment was not far away when he passed his manuscript to Hofrath Moritz, who declared, "this is no unknown writer. It is Goethe, Herder or

Wieland [and that] it was above Goethe – it was something wholly new...your work is a jewel."[111]

Jean Paul's mother was very proud of her son. The novel had earned him some money but was quite a global success. Jean Paul knowing its faults decided to eventually re-write it with a more satisfactory conclusion. He never found the opportunity of doing so, however, and before he died he referred to it as a *Born Ruin*."[112] Contemporary critics praised the book for its wealth of imagination, feeling and wit, but were critical of its mannerism."[113] Dorothy Berger, referring to Eduard Berend's interpretation, stated that, "the central motif of the cave was inspired by Rousseau, who wanted to keep a child away from all the influences of its environment."[113] She continued to say that the writers Tieck, Novalis, Hoffmann, and later on Bretano, were deeply impressed by this novel."[114]

One of Germany's motifs adopted by the Romanticists was the blue flower, which made its appearance in the *Invisible Lodge*. The blue flower was often associated with Novalis, but referred to in many works of the Romantic era. It represented, the symbolic flower, "the colour of infinity, of sea, and sky and far mountains, of longing for something far off...it is [also] a longing for the past, when the flowers could speak, and for a future world which he has entered in dreams."[115]

The whole novel became very confused at points and moved quickly between different scenarios, including Jean Paul's favourite device of dreams. Dreams became reality and reality would merge back into dreams. They became a central theme to Jean Paul, having had the dream about his own death as a youth and were the recurring theme, threading their way into and through his novels. The dream he had of his own death had stayed with him, although it is also possible that the words of Prospero, from his knowledge of Shakespeare, may have also inspired his quest to understand dream sequences. In *The Invisible Lodge*, the "dream of drinking at least proves that one is truly thirsty, then man – after having taken the poetic detour through the captivating paintings of a spurned reality – returns back to reality, forever and more purely. These captivating paintings give back a more faithful friend to nature, freedom, domestic happiness, and reality than the one they abducted from them."[116]

The title of the novel had led us to believe that the story would be about a secret society, but it was only when the story was nearing its conclusion that we learned of its relevance. The subterranean cave where Gustavus had been brought up had been, afterwards, used as a meeting place for political dissenters and separatists of the state, or so we were led to believe. The author may have been a member of this secret society, as he told the reader, that "on the whole [they] steal more humorously and harmlessly than any other."[117]

By looking more deeply into the workings of the group, coupled with the title of the novel and its suggestive implications, Jean Paul could have been indicating that the 'invisible' and the 'lodge,' were members of a freemason society, likely to have had links with the Rosicrucians. The sect was represented by the Latin rose (Rosa) and the cross (crux), as symbols of Christ's resurrection and redemption. The original Rosicrucians had also been known as the 'immortals' and the 'invisibles,' Their alleged invisibility tended to be confirmed by the fact that no one had ever caught sight of a member of the elusive brotherhood."[118]

Thoughts about Masonic orders were perhaps in the mind of Jean Paul when he steered the novel towards that conclusion. The unrest in Europe at the time of his writing would have been at the front of his mind, and Jean Paul would have been very aware of the first stirrings of democracy with dissatisfaction against the Church and states of oppression. Humanity was being crushed by the three great powers of ignorance; the power of the mob, superstition; the power of the church, and fear; the power of aristocratic, cruel and powerful despots.

The Invisible Lodge, therefore, had a surprising and unsatisfactory ending. The hero Gustavus was in prison, although he was not a member of the group. There was a shot, and a confession by Ottomar, who revealed everything to Dr Fenk in order to save Gustavus. We were left with the concluding words that Gustavus was still alive, suggesting that Jean Paul would either write a second volume or re-write the original with a more satisfactory ending. The novel was never completed.

The Invisible Lodge was the first real novel written by Jean Paul, and held all the elements associated with Romanticism; the beautiful descriptions of nature, the Gothic dreams and doppelganger, the music and inner psychology of the characters, the religious and supernatural fear of ghosts. Its subjective approach indicated that Jean Paul's influences were from his own background, the people he knew and his own love of nature. The digressions and biographical details, plus the wit and humour were the unique additions that gave the novel its Jean Paul identity, making the reader his ally, and without which the novel would have just been a mirror image of others at the time.

The novel *Hesperus* (1795) presented a more complex plot, which included the themes of love and sentiment, adventures, journeys, political intrigues and, unexpectedly, Indian mysticism. According to Buckminster Lee, *Hesperus* "was the work by which the author had been best known, out of Germany," and commented that the story was "so confused that probably many persons have read and admired the book, without even getting a clear idea of it story."[119]

It was Jean Paul's second romance novel, in which he successfully gave full reign to the emotions of his characters and their impending destinies, in order to grip the attention of his readers, although, as in all works by Jean Paul, there were the usual digressions throughout.

The chapters were called *Post-Dog Days*, another invention of the author to be creative and different. In this instance he imagined that the chapters were brought to him on an island by a dog, a Pomeranian, which swam across to the island with the chapters in a basket around his neck. The image of the dog as helper and companion was continued from *The Invisible Lodge* when the dog (in the cave), was a poodle. As a continuation of *The Invisible Lodge*, *Hesperus* had many familiar characters and devices. The Genius of the previous novel was replaced by the mystic, Emanuel, who has the same loving nature and educated the children, who are again, being deceived about their birth-right. Through Emanuel, or Dahore, (his Indian name), there is the love of nature, and the seeking of God and immortality.

The whole story revolved around the love –triangle that developed between Flamin, Clotilde and Victor, although the history of the characters had many complications caused by the prince, who left five sons in different countries, followed by the exchanging of Victor (the chaplain, Eyman's son) and Flamin, (the prince's son), at birth, in one of Jean Paul's educational experiments. None of the five sons was aware of his real origins.

The two boys were joined by Julius, the blind son of Eyman and Julia, the daughter of Horion. All four were educated by Emanuel, with all the qualities of Jean Paul, who said, "Dahore had the hearts of all children in his tender hand, simply because his own never boiled and blustered, and because an ideal beauty sat upon his youthful form and an ideal love dwelt in his pure breast."[120] The children had to stay with Emanuel until they were ten to twelve years of age. The character of Emanuel represented Jean Paul's own struggle with the problem of how to face death, to the extent of choosing the appointed day and preparing his own open grave. Problems arose however that put a stop to his plans when he did not die as expected, but ironically, was knocked unconscious by an explosion and believed to be dead. In a further twist of fate following a thunder storm he recovered and believed that God had saved him. A further incident, during a further bout of unconsciousness, saw Emanuel's vision which reflected Jean Paul's own beliefs; that all souls were destroyed by one great ecstasy. It was in that cloud of confusion where mysticism, realism and pneumonia combined, that Emanuel finally died.

In a surprise twist, following their education, Flamin (the prince's son) was to be educated with the aim of his becoming an advocate, whilst Victor (the chaplain's son), was trained to become a doctor. That was the background to prepare the reader for their eventual arrival in Germany. Clotilde had returned to her father, Le Baut, on the island of St. Lune. Both Victor and Flamin fell in love with Clotilde when they saw her again. The reader had been given the information that Clotilde was aware of the situation regarding the birth of the boys, but had been sworn to secrecy. The plot developed complications of Shakespearean proportions, as Victor was honour bound not to reveal his love for Clotilde, being aware that Flamin had fallen in love with her, also.

The zealous Mattieu and his abilities to imitate sounds and voices, added to the mix, caused additional trouble and confusion for the young lovers. Knef, who was Victor's servant, and undercover to gain information about Victor, the court and the Englishmen, was finally revealed as the fifth son.

The digressions of Jean Paul as narrator are filtered throughout, until the final chapters, when he takes an active role in the proceedings. It was then that he gave a eulogy about the future, in some ways empathising with Kant's own philosophy about the constellation, but with the hope, as in Jean Paul's philosophy, of moving towards pure spirit. With all eyes on the starry sky, the Romantic constellation representing God and heaven, Jean Paul concluded that it was not what had gone before, but what was to come that was important. His message was one of love and hope, which filtered through all his works, asserting that "there must be a God, a Virtue, and an Eternity."[121]

Having only a limited range of characters, (although many more than previously) and personal experience, Jean Paul's theme relied heavily upon the moral and intellectual errors, and weaknesses of the characters. It was that which held the novel together, despite the many complications of the plot.

Buckminster Lee stated that although *Hesperus* failed "as a work of art, the aim which the author intended is, yet a temple where humanity, love and nature are reverenced. It is full of passages and whole scenes of exquisite beauty, and rich to excess in the peculiarities of our author. The passages dazzled us with wit and condensed sentences of wisdom, and the reader is fatigued by a prolonged perusal, as he is by a book of aphorisms."[122] It was, however, successful in delivering its message of love and hope, God, heaven and future in the next life, and the German readers appreciated the novel, which was a best seller in Germany.

The novel *Flower, Fruit and Thorn Pieces* (1796) was originally written in four volumes, and was Jean Paul's first full-length novel. It was a huge success, and brought both money and recognition into his life. The story followed the fortunes of his main character, Siebenkäs, and contained many themes, such as life and death, marriage and divorce, wealth and poverty. It presented the powerful dynamics of a love, ideal love, and relationships, as well as putting the spotlight on the acquisition of happiness. The outer and inner worlds of reality and fantasy collided as Siebenkas dreamed of love and riches whilst living with poverty in a loveless marriage. In fact, the novel contained many moments and incidents of humour, with the plot of who has married Lenette; Siebenkas or the doppelganger Leibgeber?

The narrator slipped out of first to third person narration, commenting upon the changing situations, as well as taking the role of Siebenkäs, and his attempts to write in order to earn money. It was a situation based upon the struggles of Jean Paul's own early life, in which he faced poverty and repeated attempts to earn money from his writing.

The characters appeared to be many but consisted mainly of the hairdresser, cobbler, and book-binder. His other main characters were his doppelganger, Leibgeber, and in the second volume, Natalie, who replaced Lenette to become the soul mate of Siebenkas. Leibgeber was present from the beginning at the wedding of Siebenkas and Lenette, and was responsible for the later creation of the death and deception scenes. His character was the alter-ego of Siebenkas, and the only difference between them was that Leibgeber had a slight limp and Siebenkas had a mole near his left ear, shaped like a tringle.

To add intrigue to the problems encountered by Siebenkas and Lenette, Jean Paul included the evil Venner, plus the character of Stiefel, the local minister, who became a third part in the marriage.

The sections of the novel were referred to as either flower, fruit or thorn pieces, which represented the separate periods of marriage and life. Jean Paul related those to the Catholic religion, "Catholics reckon fifteen mysteries in the life of Christ;

five joyful, five painful, and five glorious."[123] The novel followed that pattern; the joyful being the pre-marriage and wedding state, in which the happiness of the groom was felt, the five painful during the marriage which brought dissatisfaction and poverty, and the five glorious being the resurrection to a new life with true love.

The theme of death was a recurring one running through the novel, with Siebenkas in his highly emotive state, desiring death to the life he found himself in. His dream about the dead Christ illustrated his unconscious suffering, and anxiety about God and the question of immortality. He received the answer he had been seeking, following the disturbing dream that had consumed him, as he slept on the mountain side, waking he claimed, "my soul wept for joy, that it could again worship God; and the joy, and the tears, and the belief in him were the prayer...and between the heaven and the earth a glad fleeting world stretched out its short wings and lived like myself in the presence of the infinite Father, and from all nature around me flowed sweet peaceful tones, as from evening bells."[124] The immortality of the soul was an ongoing concern for Jean Paul in all his works.

J.W. Smeed stated that, "from the Romantics onwards, the dream has been used to examine the dreamer's character, to hint at future events or to show how past events work on the dreamer's imagination, to reflect a state of confusion or of premonition, a period of stock-taking or a turning point."[82] In the case of Siebenkas the dreams were his attempt to free himself from his restrictions and escape into a freer existence.

In many of Jean Paul's works there was the desire to find his ideal woman, but he usually digressed on the point of women, and not always in a good way, although they were often laced with wit and humour, "the eternal wagging of a woman's tongue is to assist in shaking and jolting the atmosphere, which would otherwise become putrid [and with their] tea and coffee it was soon found…this fluid proved rather advantageous than otherwise to female gossip."[126]

The main story of his marriage to Lenette illustrated how the differences of character between husband and wife could lead to problems, Lenette, a simple, down-to-earth woman with her own hat-making business, could not understand Siebenkas his literary world and the book he was writing, which was the *Devil's Papers*. The only book she owned was her cookery book, and her passion was cleaning, which she did continuously. The pain she suffered turned to stress, washing her hands repeatedly up to forty times a day, a condition in modern times that would be called occupational compulsive disorder. However, the representation of it was a symbolic display of the tension created in the relationship between Lenette and Siebenkas.

Although she tried to please Siebenkas, it had the opposite effect, leading to misery for them both, particularly when they had to sell their possessions. The stigma of poverty made the gap between them deeper, and Lenette, who was religious and staunch Lutheran, was ashamed that they had no goose for St.Martin's Day.

The novel created a powerful and psychological insight into the minds of its characters, being very atmospheric, in which the reader could 'feel' the tension between the characters, and which, eventually, led to tragedy. The breakdown of the marriage led Siebenkas to reflect that, "the engagement day is love's longest. After that the devil collects, well, not everything, but everyday yet another piece. The velvet string of marriage binds the poetic wings, and the marriage bed is for fantasy a Castel Saint' Angelo and a detention room with water and bread…marriage covers over the poetic world with the rind of the real world."[127]

The novel did balance the sadness of the plot with lighter moments of comic-humour, particularly the catching of Venner, and later, with the fake-death scenes.

When Siebenkas had left Lenette, with thoughts about divorce, he discovered Natalie, who was the personification of his 'ideal' woman. Because of the complications about his identity, Siebenkas undertook a teaching post destined never to see her again.

Suffering and love were the two main themes of the second volume, as Siebenkas still loved his wife, who was with Stiefel, but had also lost Natalie. Siebenkas and Natalie met again at the graveside of Lenette, symbolising the passing of one love and the finding of new love. The symbolic rose and its thorns and bleeding wound, images of the death and resurrection of Christ, which suggested that love was eternal and could triumph over death, reinforced by Natalie's words, "eternity is upon earth!"[128] Jean Paul's conclusion must have satisfied his female readers with the images of this message, and by the reunion of the lovers, at the end.

According to Mrs Lee, the novel, "was one of the most personal of all Jean Paul's works,"[129] with its reconstruction of his own life, as he moved from a simple rustic life, through poverty, to develop his ideals of poetry and the imagination. It brought admiration and respect, "from poor country school-masters and pastors, the class of persons that he had described with such simplicity and naivety, begging him to lend or give a copy of some of his works, and perhaps more welcome yet, …fifty Prussian dollars and the following letter:

"You should be poor, Herr Richter, you! The millionaire in understanding, as such are usually poor; and this is right, for the others write no books; and as your books give me satisfaction, very great satisfaction, I hold myself indebted to Herr Richter, and would give him a little proof that his readers are grateful. Many readers cannot show their gratitude, and that also is well, or Herr Richter would become rich, and write no more books…Your grateful and devoted, Septimus Fixlien. The writer remained unknown until many years after, when a happy accident revealed him to Richter."[130]

Mrs Lee added that "it is impossible to present an analysis or abstract of this remarkable work. The Germans gave it a philosophical and poetical interpretation. They say that Jean Paul intended to represent Siebenkas as dying to the actual, to the everyday life of man; and in the reluctant and bleeding heart with which he tears himself away from Lenette, is meant to be represented the great struggle of the soul to rise to a higher, an ideal life."[131]

Jean Paul, in the *Preface* (letter to my friends) of his novel *Life of Quintus Fixlien*, (1796), stated that the aim of the story was about being happier (not happy), and that "we ought to value little joys more than great ones."[132] He went on to illustrate his point with many examples, in the Jean Paul style of illusion and metaphor. The quest for happiness was an ongoing on for Jean Paul.

The chapters in this novel he called letter boxes, and there were fifteen of them! It was a warm, sentimental and biographical novel, offering images such as those he retained of his own mother, ironing and cooking dinner, "you can figure how this true, warm-hearted mother may have lain in wait all morning for her schoolman whom she loved as the apple of her eye."[133] Fixlein, as in Jean Paul's own life, was "bound for the church,"[134] following in his father's footsteps. The small everyday events were portrayed through blissful rose-coloured glasses. Quintus had been brought up with Thiennette (Stephanie), the heroine and love- object, we learn about very early in the story, and follow the progress of their relationship.

As in *Hesperus*, there was the mention again of India, and its Pagodas, which represented the "temple and the god,"[135] with further reference to the council house being like an "India-house, where not only resolutions or appointments, but also shoes and cloth, are exposed to sale."[136]

The musical references of tone and sound, together "represented love and hope" for Jean Paul.[94] The musical background was a regular device in the works of the Romantics, but formed an essential part in the works of Jean Paul, who was also a very talented musician.

The novel of *Quintus Fixlien* contained a mixture of humour tinged with sadness when the character of Quintus had the honour of Conrectorate conferred on him, unfortunately for the wrong reasons; he was expected to die early, at thirty-two years old, as had the other generations of his family. As the church records had been destroyed in a fire at the church, nobody could say for certain how old Quintus was, and all assumed he was younger. Theinnette mistook Quintus's offer of half his fortune on his death as a proposal of marriage. When he realised it, and thought she would die from blood loss, he realised that he had to marry her, considering that he would be dying anyway.

Quintus attempted to persuade the Rittmeister to let him become Parson of Hukelum, his childhood home. He had everything he had always wanted, but death and the fear of it, was always hanging over him. In chapter eleven the narration changed from third to first person, and Jean Paul became godfather to the baby, who was also to be named Jean Paul.

Sadness loomed when our narrator, under guise of being the biographer to Quintus discovered, in the old toy box of his brother, a reminder of happy childhood times, and the temporary nature of existence. A memorial written by his father, giving the dates of the boys' birth confirmed Quitus to be thirty two years old on the day of his son's baptism. Despite attempts to keep it away from him, Quintus discovered the memorial for himself. He tried to shut out the thoughts going around in his head, and even had a dream, seeing himself dead. We know from his autobiography that Jean Paul actually had the same dream.

The story merged into the Romanticists' view of death, with Quintus's vision being of his place in the afterlife. Quintus thought he would die through a psychological self-fulfilling prophecy, he expected it to become reality. The self-deception made him physically ill. By psychological tricks from the other characters, he was made to realise that there was nothing wrong with him and that he was not going to die. It was a good example of how the power of the mind could easily be influenced, and that it was love and hope, the philosophy of Jean Paul, not fate, that hovered over life and death.

It also led to the realisation that his life was ideal and real, and that instead of chasing other higher ideals, life should be lived for the present and not the future, reinforced by the philosophy of Jean Paul, that "little joys refresh us constantly like house-bread, and never bring disgust; and great ones, like sugar bread, briefly… despise anxiety and wishing, the Future and the Past…enjoy thy existence more than thy Manner of Existence, and let the dearest object of thy Consciousness be this Consciousness itself."[137]

The Campaner Thal or Discourses on the Immortality of the Soul (1797), was an artistic masterpiece, with its breathtaking visions of the Pyrenees and surrounding areas. The background and scenery of nature's wonderful produce in the novel, gave support to the arguments put forward about life after death, and as Mrs Lee commented, it was "one of the most serious and poetically beautiful of the entire author's minor works."[138]

The area discussed in the novel was the Campan, defined as being an "Anti-Heaven between Ante-Hells,"[139] in the Pyrenees. Jean Paul's novel took him through an imaginary journey through France to Spain. The structure of the novel/journal was a series of letters to his friend Victor, that Jean Paul referred to as 'stations.' He began the novel at the 501st station, July, 1796.

Once again, the action of the novel had Jean Paul at the heart of it. Although it was classed as a novel, *The Camper Thal* was a mixture of essay and dialogue, as Jean Paul initiated the philosophical discussion about immortality with his group of friends, Karlson, the baron Wilhelmi, his wife, wife's sister and their chaplain. Karlson had been in love with Gione but she had chosen to marry the baron, despite loving Karlson.

As in the *Invisible Lodge*, there was music. At the Inn where they were to celebrate the wedding, they discovered that the funeral of the Inn Keeper's daughter was taking place, with the sadness of a funeral march alongside dancing music, which created "double music sounds in his ears."[140]

Later, the group were in a happier scene, as they "all stood under the spring music of flutes and pipes, and harps and warbling, which were living around us, with and without wings."[141] Even when the wedding party prepared to travel, the bride had taken her guitar. The Campan Cave was a reminder of the *Invisible Lodge*, but was "the largest and most beautiful Cave!" with its "crystal sides, shining like an illuminated ice Louvre, a gleaming sub-terrestrial heaven vault."[142]

Man and nature, the essential aspect of Jean Paul's narrative, were the consistent aspects of the novel, with descriptive and visual images as though painted by an artist, "the lily-chafer hung like gold embroidery on the pale, ripe roses, long-legged shining gnats ran glittering over the thorns; the flower-divers and nectary treasure-diggers, the bees, covered the rose-cups with new thorns; the butterflies, like moving tints – like epicurean colours, gently floated round the branch's gay world."[143]

Jean Paul used the scenes of nature as subjects for his musical appreciation when he remarked to the chaplain, "the temple of nature had been changed into a concert-hall for me, and every vocal into instrumental music."[144]

The main theme of the novel, the immortality of the soul, is discussed with the chaplain, who was a disciple of Kant, and claimed the belief that "emigrants from the earth will visit every planet, and those delicate souls who shun the sun will find themselves happy in Uranus; that the widely differing climates in the planets was no conclusion against the future residence of man upon them, because man can accommodate himself to every climate."[145]

Jean Paul's thoughts turned to Romantic nature; the flowers and the insects, and he concluded, in his attempt to prove a case for immortality, that "the Rhine rushes like a giant from its summit, disperses in the fog, falls as rain upon the plain, then it forms itself into clouds, and roams over the sands, and carries suns instead of rainbows."[146] On the negative side he admitted, the "simultaneous decay and destruction of the body and of the soul; secondly, the absolute impossibility of ascertaining the mode of life of a future existence, or as the chaplain would say, to see into the spiritual world from the sensual one."[147]

Jean Paul considered how many people accepted the belief of life after death and that, "on the whole, I find fewer men than one would imagine, who decidedly believe in, or deny, the existence of a future world...the majority, according to the promptness of alternating feelings, waver poetically between both beliefs."[148]

He concluded that "we bear in our own breasts a heaven full of constellations. There is in our heart an inward spiritual world, that breaks like a sun upon the clouds of the outward world...that inward universe of goodness, beauty, and truth."[149]

The conclusion offered by Jean Paul, made from feeling rather than academic questioning, was one of love and hope.

"The more tenderly and warmly one loves, so much more does he discover in himself defects rather than charms...thus our little faults first made known to us when we have ascended the higher steps of religion. The more we satisfy the demands of conscience, the stronger they become. Love and religion are here like the sun, by mere daylight and torchlight, the air of the apartment is pure and undisturbed, but let in a sunbeam, and how much dust and motes are hovering about."[150]

He continued the theme of immortality much later in his life with the novel *Selina*. The main character, Selina was the daughter of Gione, who was the reflection and embodiment of her mother, and had won the admiration of Jean Paul for her interest and empathy with him. Although he had lost his eyesight at the time, he had dictated to his friend Otto, who, according to Mrs Lee, placed the *Campaner Thal* upon the coffin of Jean Paul, before he too, died. *The North American Review* stated that it "is known to all readers of Jean Paul's life, that he was engaged on a work resuming the subject of *The Campaner Thal*, when death arrested the busy hand and brain, and took that great heart home to the perfection for which it yearned and laboured. It was this unfinished work, the '*Selena*,' and not *The Campaner Thal*, which was laid upon his coffin, and went down with all that was mortal of Jean Paul into his grave."[151]

Titan (1800), was an elaborate extension of Jean Paul's novels, in which there were familiar plots, twists and turns. It was not always an easy novel to read, and could be confusing, but as Jean Paul referred to it as his masterpiece, and others have since called it so, then it warranted further examination to establish the reasons for it to be heralded as such a superior story.

There were far more characters interacting in *Titan*, all with their own personalities and agendas than in other works. Journeys, exotic locations, and the favourite location of the island was employed, but the most important aspect of any Jean Paul novel was the psychology of his creations; the characters, and the eternal power of nature. The women; Linda, Liana and Idoine had strong, but very defined characteristics; their personalities and appearances described with the eye of an artist.

Maurice Cross pointed out in his review that Jean Paul, "has a whole imaginary geography of Europe in his novels. It is indeed a mighty maze; and often the panting reader toils after him in vain, or, baffled and spent, indignantly stops short, and retires…let us not run from him after the first cursory glance…there are rays of the keenest truth, nay, steady pillars of scientific light rising through this chaos. Richter requires more study than most readers care to give…we see confusion more and more unfold itself into order [becoming] a vast magnificent, and variegated scene…glittering in the brightest and kindest sun."[152]

The title was taken from the ancient Titans who fought the gods. Jean Paul had read some of the Greek mythological stories in his youth and took his images from them. Jean Paul took the basic ideas and, according to Mrs Lee, they evolved into "the limitations and compensations of life – all power, as soon as it aims to exceed its just bounds, breaks down; that all who would violate the laws of eternal justice, necessarily fail."[153] The moral implications of the novel in many ways reflected the concerns of the age in which he was writing.

Although Jean Paul intended to give *Titan* the "tragic-comic character of his other works, and that the comic should enter largely into its composition, his new experiences at Weimar made him re-think and he concluded that *Titan* should be a serious romance, reserving the satirical and comic for an appendix."[154]

Jean Paul wrote four volumes of *Titan*, within which, "revolves much that is great and beautiful and touching in life; almost all the errors and sorrows and pains of humanity; love, in all its forms, from the delicate fragrance, to that of the lily of the valley, to the volcanic flame that burns and destroys; nature, in the idyllic simplicity of German village life, in ornamented parks and gardens, in Alpine mountains, and in the intoxication of spring in the Italian climate; art, from the breathing tones of the flute to the noble beauty of Grecian sculpture; poetry, delicate irony, hidden satire, and broad humour."[155]

"Throughout the whole work an elevated poetic justice was preserved; not the common conventional justice that demands vice to be punished and virtue rewarded *in this world* but a deeper philosophy, in which the mind itself and the affections, though crushed and disappointed, are their own reward."[156]

Richter's purpose was to "give a lesson of humility to those who, strong in self-reliance, throw aside the guards of custom, the sanction of laws, as unnecessary to their more refined and spiritual natures."[157]

The emotional conflicts gave an added tragic intensity to the story line, as the life of Albano, the central character and hero, the Titan of the work, unfolded before our eyes. The novel charted the growth and progress of Albano from his youthful and chaotic early days to his maturity as a man.

In Jean Paul style the reader accepted, at first reading, that Gaspard was the father of Albano, but as in his other novels, the main character of Albano did not know who his real parents were, being separated from them at an early age. Our first introduction to Albano was as he was taken to the island in Lago, Maggiore. As though blind, he allowed his friends to describe the scenery to him.

When the character of Gaspard was introduced the impression was of a cold and remote personality, but who was also subtle and clever. For him, the other characters were merely tools to use for his own agenda. He did not display any emotion, making him a difficult character to pin down. The plot was developed around the idea of Albano searching for his roots, his experiences, and inner spiritual growth, to eventually find peace, although he was in fact destined for greater things.

The initial influence of Albano's separation from his parents in order to be educated, were reminiscent of those from the philosophy of Rousseau, in that Albano was classically educated and artistic. He was to receive a greater education in the area of love through the female influences of Liane, Linda and Idoïne

Albano's visit to the parents of Liane opened him to the emotions of love and beauty when he saw her half-hidden form through her window. His love for Liane was described by Jean Paul as being, "the atmosphere he breathes in, the medium through which he looks; his is the spirit which gives life and beauty to whatever it embraces."[158]

The emotional conflict was drawn together through the revelation of his female characters, all different types, and containing aspects of Jean Paul's own personality. The character of Liane was painted as a white and half-angelic creature, intelligent and uncomplaining.

She had existed in the mind of Albano long before he met her, for him she was a saint, but even then she was unable to speak to him as she was aware of his royal roots, but sworn to secrecy. From her introduction it appeared that she would eventually marry Albano, but Jean Paul had different ideas, making her suffer blindness, and cutting short her life, which may not have been received easily by his female readers.

The theme of blindness could be found in many of the novels, and was a theme frequently explored by Jean Paul. In Titan, there was the blindfold worn by

Albano, the half-visible vision of Liane, added to which was the nervous blindness suffered by Liane which led to the tragedy of her death.

Death and partings form a great deal of the novel's structure, with complications and revelations, deception and faith, being Jean Paul's effects to gain sympathy, and empathy for his characters, particularly the character of Liane, who died.

Other familiar devices were dreams, with "mystic complexity and gloom, amid the dim gigantic, half-ghastly shadows, gleamings of a wizard splendour,"[159] and the Romantic Aeolian harp playing frequently in the background.

"The infinite Night, with her solemn aspects, Day, and the sweet approach of 'Even and Morn,' were full of meaning for him. He loved the green Earth with her streams and forests, her flowery leaves and eternal skies; loves her with a sort of passion, in all her vicissitudes of light and shade; his spirit revels in her grandeur and charms; expands like the breeze over wood and lawns, over glade and dingle, stealing and giving odours."[160]

The novel ended on a positive note with Albano discovering his true roots and then finding a new love in the shape of the princess Idoine, who was Liane's double (another example of Jean Paul's literary technique using the doppelganger) and who he regarded as his true soul-mate. He was then allowed to meet his twin-sister Julienne. His older brother died leaving the way clear for Albano to undertake his role as prince, bringing political stability by uniting the two states.

The four volumes of *Titan* were published in three successive years, but because Jean Paul had changed the earlier serious romance to a later inclusion of the comic appendix, it created divisions between his reading audiences. In England, Richardson's *Clarissa* had received the same type of reception. The conclusion was that both novels had their parallel. In both cases each author was reproached by their readers to alter or conceal the fate of their heroines, but without success.

Walt and Vult (1807), was the "first work that Jean Paul began and finished immediately after his marriage, when he had obtained the object of his life-long desires."[161] Mrs Lee described it as "a series of pictures, describing the successive moods of mind of the poet; and from these moods of mind, arise, scenes of comic, tender or pathetic interest. It contained Jean Paul's own view of the value of his own art; that of an imaginative writer, and the adaptation of such a pursuit to the actual world. It probably throws more light on the personal character of the author than any other of his works."[162]

This novel was about duality in all its aspects. It reflected the dual personality of Jean Paul through his twin characters, Walt and Vult, and also contrasted the worlds of reality against that of the imagination, or the Romantic view of life. It presented all that was positive and negative in the world, as deception, truth, and innocence were pitted against each other, as well as in the character of each twin.

As a reflection of Jean Paul's own childhood, the twins were born in humble life. Because of their character disposition it was decided that Vult should be enlisted into the army, (as Jean Paul's brother was), and Walt was destined to enter the church, as Jean Paul's grandfather, father and himself were also destined. Jean Paul, as fate decreed, by chance and circumstance, became a poet, philosopher and writer. There was much in *Walt and Vult* that echoed not just the beliefs of Jean Paul, but his whole outlook on life.

Walt was the embodiment of Jean Paul with his empathy for nature, poetry, music, and the simple life, whilst Vult represented the sociable, outgoing nature, with a fondness for music, but displaying a wicked wit and humour. Psychologically, they were always in fierce competition with each other, and although it was unspoken, they would always be there to save each other from unknown situations. Even the dream sequence in volume two suggested a telepathic link, when Vult sent a letter to Walt, indicating that he knew where Walt had been, and what had happened to him. The reader was to find out later that Vult had been following Walt in order to protect him.

Walt, with his open and honest character, unexpectedly, thwarts all the potential threats against him, but accepts them as trials to be endured and vanquished. The plot of the novel traversed those 'unknown' situations, which brought the twins, unknowingly, and eventually, together.

The novel began with the reading of the will of Mr. Van der Kabel, which placed that 'situation' into context, and allowed the reader to identify the good characters from the bad. The will had made Walt the heir to property and fortune, but, complications arose when it was discovered that sixteen or more stipulations were attached, before the fortune could be collected by Walt. Walt's poem was the catalyst for the plot. The Croesus, and his cunning legacy, created the evil from which the complications of the story unravelled. The reader was made aware that the battle would become one of good versus evil.

The chapters devoted to the journey of Walt allowed Jean Paul to expand upon his favourite topic of nature, which filter throughout the story. "How beautiful it is, he wrote, in these pillared halls of nature, the living green above and beneath, an eternal succession of infinite life…Trees and flowers! Ye bow yourselves hither and thither as though you were living, and would speak to our hearts. I love you as though I were myself a flower with its blossoms. Ah! Once I lived a higher life."[163]

The journey also allowed Jean Paul to comment on children, which he was to do so more fully in his next book, *Levana*. "Ah, were I only for a little time almighty, or powerful, I would create a world especially for myself, and suspend it under the mildest sun; a little world where I would have nothing but little lovely children, and these little things I would never suffer to grow up, but only to play, eternally."[164]

The journey, whether factual or in fiction, had been a regular and constant theme by writers in the eighteenth and nineteenth centuries. It allowed the writer to give readers a more colourful view of the world from their armchairs. Jean Paul had always enjoyed travelling alone, and would perhaps have enjoyed more extensive travel than he could afford, but his use of exotic locations and the wonders of nature ooze through his works.

In *Walt and Vult*, we are told, "travelling was always to him an inexpressible satisfaction, especially if he journeyed in unknown places; for upon the way he always flattered himself that it was possible he might meet with one of those delightfully Romantic adventures, of which he yet sometimes read. The high road, that as a river ornamented the landscape, and in its infinite windings, now here now there, took his imagination with it, was it not an infinite delight to him, for it reflected the whole of life?"[165]

There was also the love-interest in the form of the beautiful princess Wina, with whom both twins fell in love. Mrs Lee suggested that "the reason that the book breaks off so abruptly is, no doubt that it would have violated all possibility, and all German conventionalism, to have brought Walt's love for Wina to a happy termination; and yet could be permitted to love nothing inferior."[166] The character of Wina "runs through the whole book like a sweet undertone, heard only at the intervals when the clang of the other instruments pauses. Or, she is like an exquisite perfume, which seems always to come to us, as if it were a *remembered sense*; evanescent, but associated with the fairest and purest hours of existence."[167]

Walt was infatuated with Wina, and had been for many years since they were children. When he attended the concert he referred to his search for her, "how could he find a diamond in a field covered with sparkling dew drops?"[168]

Music was another staple theme in the story, being "the interpreter between the present and the future."[169] No work by Jean Paul was complete without the sounds of music in the background, or, even brought to the reader's attention, or by his descriptions of the various instruments, which gave greater emotion to particular scenes. Through the words of Vult music was referred to as being, "of all the arts the most purely human, the universal art."[170] Walt's attendance at the music concert described the different sounds and the effects they had upon the listener, "Oh, pure, unspotted music! How holy is thy joy and thy pain! They jubilee and thy sounds of woe are not for any one circumstance in life, but for life, for existence itself."[171] Jean Paul later commented that "Mozart was a musical Shakespeare."[172]

Dorothy Berger suggested that the "purpose of the novel[Walt and Vult] was to achieve a synthesis of the two characters; the development of Walt towards maturity, with a realistic view of this world, even to the point of hating somebody, and of Vult's giving in to his love for to whom he belongs, freeing himself of the dangerous isolation that leads characters like Schoppe, Giannozzo, and himself, to self-destruction."[173] As in all works, Jean Paul's story ends on a hopeful note in which "Walt is left, still aspiring to the reach the highest; the *ideal* is still before him – and the reader is left with hope, that he will not forever wait at the gate of paradise."[174]

The publication of *Levana, Or the Doctrine of Education* (1807) was followed by the Battle of Jena, where Germany was defeated by Napoleon. Jean Paul claimed that defeat would not have happened "if the battle had been fought with the pen,"[175] and that "his prophetic feeling told him at that time, what better experience has taught the nations of Europe, that all must unite in the common cause of freedom, and that *one* without the rest could not advance in the road to civilization and better government. He held the depression of the hopes and spirits of the people as one of the greatest evils of all time."[176]

Jean Paul campaigned against the taxes to support the war effort, and wrote many political essays giving hope to his people, who eventually rose up against Napoleon to reclaim their country. After Levana, Jean Paul returned to writing in the comedy style, producing *Dr. Katzenberger's Journey to a Spa* and *Army-Chaplain Schmeltz Journey to Flatz*, aiming to help raise the spirits of the German people.

Jean Paul dedicated the *Levana* to Caroline, Queen of Bavaria, on behalf of all mothers. He admitted that he had not read everything about education, but pointed out that Rousseau's *Emile* had been his inspiration, claiming, "no work can be compared to his [and that] the spirit of education which fills and animates the work has shaken to their foundations and purified all the school-rooms and even the nurseries in Europe. In no previous education work on education was the ideal so richly and beautifully combined with actual observation as in his."[177]

The *Levana* had been Jean Paul's first scientific work, and was very successful in Germany. "Even Goethe forgot his hostility to the author, and seeing an extract from the work, wrote to a friend, "I know not how to say enough of this extract from *Levana*, and desire with impatience the whole work."[178] His philosophy had been to "liberate…the ideal human being which lies concealed in every child,"[179] preface by making them think spiritually, originally and creatively through intellectual pursuits, placing the importance upon the individuality of each child. Jean Paul regarded the *Levana* as his "most serious production, to which only a short, occasional comic Appendix shall be added."[180] The comic appendix was of a dreamed letter to the late

Professor Gellert, in which he discussed finding an 'ideal' tutor, giving his beliefs about teachers and children's educational needs.

Religion, God, truth and morality were the supporting issues behind the Levana's educational curriculum. Jean Paul questioned "if a whole system of religious metaphysics did not dreamingly sleep within the child, how could the mental contemplation of infinity, God, eternity, holiness &c, be imparted to him, since we cannot communicate it by outward means, and indeed have nothing for that purpose but words, which have not the power of creating, but only of amusing? The dying and the fainting hear inward music which no outward object gives and ideas are such inward tones."[181] He claimed that spiritual education should begin at birth, with the most important and relevant statement of the child being taught to "receive different religions as lovingly as different languages, in which but one spirit of humanity is expressed. Every genius is all-powerful in his own language, every heart in its own religion."[182]

According to Timothy Casey, "Jean Paul remained a rationalist to the end, as he was religious from the beginning. He had much to find fault with in the Enlightenment for its lack of religious sentiment…in one of his last letters, he deplores the newest age, which brings us, instead of light, a chaotic infusion of Indian-poetic-mystical-supercredulous Christianity…he had a horror of Protestant orthodoxy, not to say of Catholicism, and the bitterest blow was the religious melancholy of his son Max, whom he tried to influence by way of models – Lessing, Kant, Jacobi, Hamann and Herder – who represented the kind of religion and the kind of enlightenment he favoured."[183]

Jean Paul's *Levana* was written from a masculine perspective with its gendered comments. He inferred throughout that mothers, indeed the entire female race, gave out the wrong treatment, information and advice to their children. Father's however, because they could speak (not 'talk like parrots,' as Jean Paul suggested), use less emotion and far fewer words, are better at educating their children. As for discipline, Jean Paul stated that "women can scarcely say to a child, 'Be quiet!' without colon and semicolon, and most necessary notes of interrogation and exclamation!"[184] He continued his tirade against women by claiming, "was there ever in history an instance of a woman training a dog? Or could a general-ess, in commanding her marching army to halt, ever express herself otherwise than thus, 'all you people, as soon as I have done speaking, I command you all to stand still in your places, halt, I tell you.'"[185]

Jean Paul had many female friends and admirers in his time, and had always made comments about the female personality in his works. The *Levana* proved to be no exception. He had looked, listened and memorized the various personality traits of the women he had met, successfully incorporating them into his characters, with depth and insight. Some of the women he treated with respect, whilst being cold and contemptuous to others.

Music was an area in which Jean Paul had always been happy. In the Levana he said, that "music, rather than poetry, should be called the happy art,"[186] and that music could be applied to soothe all moods and tempers. Coupled with singing and dancing Jean Paul must have been recalling his own happy childhood when he stated, "a father who has an old piano, or fiddle, or flute, or an improvising singing voice, should call his own and neighbour's children together, and let them everyday for an hour hop and turn by his orchestra, in pairs, in rows, in circles, very frequently alone, accompanying themselves with singing as their own grinding organ, and also in anyway they like…in the child happiness dances [and] like physical poetry exercises and equalizes all the muscles."[187]

After a great deal of sermonizing, Jean Paul addressed the question about children and "what are children really?" He referred to a poem he had written called *The Last Day*, in which the innocence of children was contrasted with the sin of Adam and Eve in the Garden of Eden. Two children were sent to Earth from Heaven after the end of the world. The question they asked was "look kindly upon us, ye parents, and do not hurt us, and play with us a long, long time, and tell us many tales, and kiss us."[188] Jean Paul's message that 'children' were innocent, and that it was by treating them wrongly that evil, instead of goodness, could develop, was a very powerful conclusion, and an educational one for adults and parents. As in most of Jean Paul's works he ends on a positive note that the past should not reflect the future, but that with the future there should be a new beginning.

Army –Chaplain Schmelzle's Journey to Flätz, and *Dr Katzenberger's Journey to a Spa* (1809), were written during the French occupation, and as comedies, they were written to bring some warmth and humour into the lives of the German people. Dr Katzenberger's character was of the detached and analytical observer, whose thoughts were of the absurd and grotesque. Normality and perfection were two words which were not in his vocabulary, whilst *Army-Chaplain Schmelzle's* was a short story about an Army Chaplain's incident-packed journey to the town of Flätz, and to which Jean Paul referred to as "a golden harvest-field of satire."[189] The novel had all the hallmarks of Laurence Sterne's *Sentimental Journey*, with its witty observations of people and places.

The plot revolved around the rumours of Attila Schmelzle's cowardice, and so he sent himself on a journey to prove his critics wrong. Full of humour, the reader followed Schmelzle and laughed at his antics, as he attempted to solve problems and make decisions, and to restrain his imagination from working overtime.

The atmosphere of Schmelzles's journey was one of suspense, as the Chaplain encountered new and quirky characters that were viewed through unchristian, but comic eyes. Ironically, it was the Chaplain who found himself the chief suspect of a robbery, had it not been for the courage of his wife in defending him. Schmelzle was a weak and cowardly character who was contrasted by a strong other-half; his wife.

This story was the only one in which women were shown in a good light, without the verbal criticisms they were usually attacked with by Jean Paul. The character of Bergelchen, the wife of Schmelzle, was a strong, loyal character, and the opposite of the often weak husband. She was his security both in mind and body, and Schmelzle even tied himself to her when in bed, so that if he walked in his sleep she could guide him back to bed. His brother-in-law acted as his bodyguard, although he waded into any dispute, before considering the situation. His great sense of humour was displayed with the bedroom 'ghost' antics, which were child-like and innocent, but proved too much for Schmelzle, who had an innate sense and fear of all things ghostly.

The dominating theme was of courage, not always in the field of war, although there were references to it, but in everyday encounters. The delights of a journey brought fear of what could happen, particularly during a thunder storm, as the imagination of Schmelzle (Jean Paul) ran amok. The scrutiny of his fellow passengers brought hilarity but also underlying questions about their personalities, displaying a tolerant contempt for the people around him.

Opposite courage there was the characteristic of cowardice, admitted to by the author, and which created some lighter moments that readers could identify with. Jean Paul's fear of ghosts was incorporated into the story with hilarious results, being the victim of a prank by his wife and brother.

The story was laced with humour from start to finish, which was the aim of Jean Paul, as he tried to bring some light relief into the lives of the German people, who were, at that time, involved in the Holy Wars.

As in all works by Jean Paul there is the question of man and his existence, heaven against the chaos of the world. It was no surprise that in the conclusion Jean Paul's thoughts turned to the end of the world, by nations employing chemical weapons, and lamented that "I wish I had that Ferment out of my head,"[190] suggesting that fear can breed fear.

His additional note that, "my brother-in-law has kept his promise well, and Berga is dancing," offered a lighter note on which the 'journey' ended, indicating that life was the here and now, and "to find reluctantly the ordinary smallness of humour nature while one sublimely hovers midway between pain and elevation above such smallness – to express this is called humour, which offers the appearance of the sublime and of the comic next to one another."[191]

Reminiscences of the Best Hours of Life for the Hour of Death (1813) was a work which was difficult to categorise, as it was short, comprising of only fifty pages. It could not have been classed as a novel or even a novellen, as it was more a brief reflection about the process of dying, a subject which frequently occupied the thoughts of Jean Paul.

The piece began with his friend Herder, who was dying, asking his son for "a great thought, that I may quicken myself with it."[192] Jean Paul reflected that it was difficult to find words of hope to someone who was dying, or anything cheerful that could make the dying person feel, not better, but comforted somehow. When faced with a dying person it is difficult to find such words, as the living are still wrapped up in their own grief, at losing someone they cared for. Jean Paul stated that dying becomes not about the person themselves any more, but about the concerns of the priests, lawyers and doctors, not to mention the relatives who will be left with the remains of body and soul. For them the death bed is, as Jean Paul pointed out, "a coffin without a lid."[193]

Jean Paul commented that it was reflections of life and the sharing of memories which could bring some comfort and solace to the dying person, who, although bodily incapable they still had, the power of the mind, although "we can by no means know how high these sensations of dying may reach."[194]

The 'story' then turned to the character of Gottreich, the son of a curate, who lived in the village of Heim. Jean Paul's character of Gottreich was a budding poet, taking after his father, who also had the same talent as a youth, but being born at a time when the talents of poets were not recognised or encouraged. The respected professions for middle-class young men with any talent, was in the law or the clergy. Jean Paul reflected that the clergy were fortunate as they were surrounded by "religion, poetry, and the life of a shepherd of souls."[195] Gottreich and his father had a good relationship, because of the similarities of interest and occupation, which echoed Jean Paul's own life.

The introduction of Justa brought love and happiness for Gottreich, who "reposed in such tenderness of bliss and love, of poetry and religion, of spring-time, of the past and of the future, that he feared, in the bottom of his heart, to speak his happiness out save in prayer."[196] The question about death was a recurring one in the novels of Jean Paul, and so the theme occurred when he reflected upon his ageing father and then with thoughts about his own mortality. He concluded that the memories of his present life and happiness would sustain him at his final hour, and had kept a written account in order to recall those memories, and which he termed, '*Reminiscences of the best hours of life for the hour of death.*'

With the onset of the Holy War (1813-14), Gottreich had enlisted in the army to fight for his country. After liberation, as he returned to Heim. He had a premonition when he looked to the mountains, which made him recall his 'reminiscences.' When he arrived home he discovered his father dying. Gottreich decided to read the 'reminiscences' to his father, who asked, "say something rich in love to me of God and his works."[197] The passages written by Gottreich were very powerful, poetical and comforting, viewing death as a new world of "eternal spring-time."[156] Jean Paul's own philosophy of immortality was incorporated into the passage, with the reference to that, as "the body crumbles away in the pains and pleasures of the flesh…souls like marsh lights [will rise] and shine in the storm and the rain [will be] unextinguishable."[198] The image of the sun represented God at the final moments, "and in his soul there stood nothing but the one sun-God!" followed by the three rainbows "over the evening sun,"[199] which was the image of the Holy Trinity, followed by, "I must go after the sun and pass through with him." It was at that point that he died.

'*Reminiscences of the Best Hours of Life for the Hour of Death* combined the life of Jean Paul, with his philosophy of death and immortality, in a short effective and emotional story. It's unique format created an interesting approach to death and the dying, but included elements of hope through reminiscences of happier times, as well as the belief in God and the eternal life.

The novels of Jean Paul presented a rich tapestry of imagination, character and events. They could make the reader both laugh and cry, and could be read and re-read, and yet always reveal some new pieces to treasure. The extra leaves and digression material alone could have occupied a book on their own. The facts, figures and snippets of information given by Jean Paul made the novels a worthwhile investment.

Aesthetically, the novels were much more than characters and plot. They contained artistic and dramatic landscapes captured by Jean Paul in all their moods and colours, and hues. Many scenes also captured the atmosphere with their additional musical accompaniment.

Endnotes:

1. Neuburg, Victor E, *Popular Literature:A History and Guide* (U.S.A: The Woburn Press, 1977), p.103

2. Routh, J., & Wolff J., (Eds.,) *The Sociology of Literature: Theoretical Approaches* (Staffordshire: Keele University of 1977), p.112

3. Eagleton, Terry, *Literary Theory: an Introduction* (2nd ed.), (Oxford: Blackwell Publishers Ltd, 1996), p.117

4. Black, J, Porter, R, (Eds.,) *A Dictionary of Eighteenth Century History* (London: Basil Blackwell, 1994), p.522

5. Baldick Chris, *Oxford Concise Dictionary of Literary terms* (Oxford: Oxford University Press, 1991), p.153

6. Bennett, E.K. *A History of the German Novelle from Goethe to Thomas Mann* (Cambridge: Cambridge University Press, 1949)

7. Blackall Eric, E.A, *The Novels of the German Romantics* (London: Cornell University Press, 1983), p.67

8. Bennett, p.4

9. Bennett, p.5

10. Bennett, p.7

11. Bennett, p.7

12. Bennett, p.15

13. Bennett, p.4

14. Bennett, p.5

15. Bennett, p.5

16. Bennett, p.8

17. Bennett, p.9

18. Bennett, p.11

19. Bennett, p.11

20. Bennett, p.13

21. Bennett, p.14

22. Furst Lilian, *Romanticism* (London: Methuen, 1979), p.2

23. Lovejoy, Arthur, O, in Halsted, John B (Ed), *Romanticism: Problems of Definition, Explanation, and Evaluation* (Boston: D.C. Heath and Company, 1965), p.40

24. Kipperman Mark, *Beyond Enchantment: German Idealism and English Romantic Poetry* (Philadelphia: University of Pennsylvania Press, 1986), p.6

25. Lovejoy, p.99

26. Drabble, Margaret, (Ed), *Oxford Companion to English Literature* (Oxford: Oxford University Press, 1985), p.604

27. Berlin Isaiah, *The Roots of Romanticism* (U.S.A: Princeton University Press, 1999), p.140

28. Berlin, p.153

29. Botting Fred, Gothic (London: Routledge, 1996), p.5

30. Norton, Rictor, (Ed,) *Gothic Readings: The First Wave 1764-1840* (London: Leicester University Press, 2000), p.vii

31. Botting Fred, *Gothic* (London: Routledge, 1996), p.5

32. Defoe Daniel, *The Novels and Miscellaneous Works of Daniel Defoe*; *The History and Reality of Apparitions* (Oxford: London Talboys, 1840), p55.

33. Defoe, p.100

34. Defoe, p.101

35. Defoe, p.105

36. Defoe, p.124

37. Defoe, p.130

38. Vidler, Alec, R, *The Church in an Age of Revolution* (London: Penguin, 1990), p.12

39. Vidler, p.31

40. Vidler, p.32

41. Vidler, p.35

42. Black, Jeremy, & Porter, Roy, *A Dictionary of Eighteenth Century History*

(London: Penguin, 1996), p.566

43. Stahl, E.L & Yuill. W.E, *German Literature in the 18th & 19th Centuries* (London:

Cresset Press, 1970), p.xxi

44. Bevis Matthew, *Comedy: A Very Short Introduction* (Oxford: Oxford University Press, 2013), p.21

45. Hazlitt William, *Lectures on the Comic Writers* (New York: Derby & Jackson, 1857), p.7

46. Hill Carl, *The Soul of Wit* (Lincoln & London: University of Nebraska Press,

1993), p.1

47. Hill, p.2

48. Hill, p.11

49. Hill, p.51

50. Taggart Caroline, *A Classical Education* (London: Michael O'Mara Books Limited, 2009), p.128

51. Hodgart Matthew, *Satire* (London: Weidenfeld and Nicolson, 1969), p.7

52. Hodgart, p.115

53. Pollard, Arthur, *Satire:The Critical Idiom* (London: Methuen & Co Ltd, 1976), p.1

54. Pollard, p.3

55. Pollard, p.2

56.Wernaer, Robert M. *Romanticism and the German Romantic School*

(http://www.jstor.org/stable/25106805)

57. Rousseau, Je an-Jacques, *Thoughts on Different Subjects* (London: Crowder, Coote, Griffin & Lock, 1768), p.59

58. Richter, Jean Paul, Buckminster Lee, Eliza, trans., *Walt & Vult*, vol: 1 (U.S.A, Boston: Charles C. Little & James Brown, 1842), p.123/4

59. Blanning, p.153

60. Berger, p.76

61. Berger Dorothea, *Jean Paul Friedrich Richter* (New York: Twayne Publishers, 1972), p.59

62. Mason, p.178

63. Mason, p.180

64. Mason, p.182

65. Mason, p.184

66. Stevens David, *Romanticism* (Cambridge: Cambridge University Press, 2004), p.44

67. Abrahams Gerald, *The Age of Beethoven* (New York: Oxford University Press, 1982), p.vi

68. Abrahams, p.ix

69. Garland, Henry & Mary, *Oxford Companion to German Literature* (Oxford: Clarendon Press, 1976), p.67

70. Samson Jim, *The Cambridge History of Nineteenth-Century Music* (Cambridge: Cambridge University Press, 2002), p.118

71. Rolland Romain, *Goethe and Beethoven* (New York/London: Benjamin Blom, 1968), p.xiip

72. Rolland, p.6

73. Rolland, p.47

74. Halstead, John B, *Problems in European Civilization: Romanticism: Problems of Definition, Explanation, and Evaluation (Welleck),* (Boston: D.C.Heath And Company, 1965), p.45-52

75. De Quincy, Thomas, *Essays on Philosophical Writers and Other Men of Letters* (*volume 1*), (Boston: Ticknor, Reed & Fields, 1853), p.180/9

76 Collins, George Stuart, *Selections From the Works of Jean Paul Friedrich Richter* (New York: Cincinnati: Chicago: American Book Company, 1898) p.136

77. Stahl, E. L, & Yuill, W.E, *German Literature in the 18th & 19th Centuries* (London: The Cresset Press, 1970), p.109

78. Webber, Andrew J, *The Doppelganger : Double Visions in German Literature* (Oxford: Oxford University Press, 1996), 57

79. Fleming Paul, *The Pleasures of Abandonment: Jean Paul and the Life of Humour.*
(New York: Königshausen & Neumann, 2005), p.19

80. Casey, T, *Jean Paul: a Reader* (Baltimore & London: The John Hopkins
University, 1992), p.6

81. Buckminster Lee, Eliza, *Life of Jean Paul Friedrich Richter, vol1*, (U.S.A, Boston:
Charles C. Little & James Brown, 1842), p.149

82. Buckminster Lee, p.149

83. Berger, Dorothea, *Jean Paul Friedrich Richter* (New York: Twayne Publishers,
1972), p.101

84. Jean Paul Richter, *The Horn of Oberon* (Detroit: Wayne State University Press,
1973), p.1. Introduction

85. Buckminster Lee, p.126

86. Fleming Paul, p.59

87. Buckminster Lee, p.125

88. Buckminster Lee, p.126

89. Buckminster Lee, p.139

90. Buckminster Lee, p.275/6

91. Black, Jeremy & Porter Roy, *A Dictionary of Eighteenth Century History*
(London: Penguin Books, 1994), p.316

92. Richter, Jean Paul, & Engel, J.J, *Maria Wuz and Lorenz Stark,* (U.S.A, Memphis:
General Books LLC, 2012), p.7

93. Richter & Engel, p.7

94. Casey, p.82

95. Buckminster Lee, p.276

96. Buckminster Lee, p.277/8

97. Webber, p.63

98. Berger, p.38

99. Richter, Jean Paul, *The Invisible Lodge* (New York: Henry Holt & Co., 1883), p.7

100. Richter, p.22

101. Richter, p.23

102. Richter, p.102

103. Richter, p.285

104. Richter, p.63

105. Richter, p.84

106. Larrissy Edward, *The Blind and Blindness in Literature of the Romantic Period* (Edinburgh: Edinburgh University Press, 2007), p.2

107. Larrissy, p.89

108. Richter, p.47

109. Richter, p.390

110.Richter, p.191

111. Buckminster Lee, p.279

112. Buckminster Lee, p.281

113. Buckminster Lee, p.288

114. Buckminster Lee, p.278

115. Berger, p.39

116. Berger, p.39

117. Smeed, J.W, *Jean Paul's Dreams* (Oxford: Oxford University Press, 1966), p.9

118. Fleming, p.40

119. Richter, p.39

120. Black, Jeremy, p.649

121. Lee, p.289

122. Richter, Jean Paul, F, *Hesperus, or, Forty-Five Dog Post Days* (U.S.A, Boston:

Ticknor & Fields, 1864), p.37

123. Richter, p.498

124. Lee, p.295/6

125. Richter, Jean Paul, *Flower Fruit & Thorn Pieces*, vol; 1(Leipzig: Bernhard

Tauchnitz, 1871), p.16

126. Richter, p. 127

127. Richter, p.284/5, vol;1

128. Smeed, J.W, *Jean Paul's Dreams* (London: Oxford University Press, 1966), p.63

129. Richter, p.173

130. Richter, Jean Paul, *Flower, Fruit & Thorn Pieces*, vol.2 (Leipzig: Bernhard

Tauchnitz, 1871), p.303

131. Richter, p.277, vol.2

132. Lee, p.304, vol;1

133. Lee, p.304/5, vol;1

134. Lee, p.306, vol; 1

135. Richter, Jean Paul, *German Romance: Richter, J.P.F: Army-Chaplain Schmelzle's*

Journey to Flatz. Life of Quintus Fixlein (Edinburgh & London: W.Tait & C.Tait,

1887) p.118

136. Richter, p.124

137. Richter, p.136

138. Richter, p.165

139. Richter, p.136

140. Richter, p.300

141. Lee, p.2 vol,2

142. Richter, Jean Paul F, *The Campaner Thal: Or, Discourses on the Immortality of the Soul* (London: Charles Gilpin, 1848), p.2

143. ibid, p.2

144. ibid, p.18

145. ibid, p.9

146. ibid, p.35

147. ibid, p.35

148. Lee Buckminster, Eliza, *Life of Jean Paul F Richter*, vol.2, (London: John Chapman, 1845), appendix, p.216

149. ibid, p.43

150. ibid, p.48

151. ibid, p.59

152. Lee, appendix, p.217

153. Lee, appendix, p.235

154. *The North American Review*, Vol: 99, No: 205, October, 1864

[URL: http://www.jstor.org/stable/25100582

155. Cross Maurice (ed.,), *Selections from the Edinburgh Review, Vol, 2* (Paris: Baudry's European Library, 1835), p.452

156. Lee Buckminster, Eliza, *Life of Jean Paul Friedrich Richter, vol: 2* (London: John Chapman, 1845), p.70

157.Lee, p.71

158.Lee, p. 76

159. Lee, p.76

160. Lee, p.76

161. Cross, p.453

162. Cross, p.457

163. Cross, p.454

164. Lee, p.85, (volume 2)

165. Lee, Preface (vol.2)

166. Richter, Walt & Vult, p.61 (volume 2)

167. Richter, p.58, (volume 2)

168. Richter, p.33, (volume 2)

169.Lee, p.85 (volume 2)

170.Lee, Preface (vol;1)

171.Richter, p.241 (vol: 1)

172.Richter, p.232 (vol;1)

173.Richter, p.257 (vol:1)

174.Richter, p.244 (vol;1)

175.Richter, p.252 (vol;1)

176.Berger, Dorothea, *Jean Paul Friedrich Richter* (New York: Twayne

Publishers, 1972), p.97

177.Richter, p.vi (Volume;1)

178. Lee, Buckminster, Eliza, *Life of Jean Paul F. Richter* p.105

179. Lee, p.105

180. Richter, Jean Paul, *Levana* (Boston: Ticknor & Fields, 1866), preface.

181. Lee, p.105

182. Richter, preface

183. Richter, p.148

184. Richter, p.59

185. Richter, p.64

186. Casey T, p.58

187. Richter, p.105/6

188. Richter, p.105/6

189. Richter, p.99

190. Richter, p.95

191. Richter, p.400

192. Richter, Jean Paul, German Romance: Army Chaplain Schmelzle's Journey to Flätz, Volume 3, (Edinburgh: W.Tait, Preface, p.27

193. p.112

194. Fleming Paul, *The Pleasures of Abandonment* (Germany: Konigshausen& Neumann, 2005), p, 19

195. Richter, Jean Paul, *Reminiscences of the Best Hours of Life for the Hour of Death* (Boston: Joseph Dowe, 1841), p.11

196. ibid, p.12

197. ibid, 14

198. ibid, 18

199. ibid, 25

200. ibid, p.39

201. ibid, 43

202. ibid, 45

203. ibid, 55

End Notes

1. Richter, Jean Paul; Introduction and translation by Margaret R Hale, *Horn of Oberon*, (Detroit: Wayne State University Press, 1973), p.xi

2. Richter, p.xvii

3.Richter, p.180

4. Richter, p.181

5. Richter, p.187

6. Richter, p.188

7. Richter, p.188

8. Richter, p.189

9. Richter, p.189

10. Richter, p.195

11. Richter, p.148

12. Richter, p.152

13. Richter, p.152

14. Richter, p.158

15. Richter, p.165

16. Richter, p.166

17. Richter, p.172

18. Richter, p.173

19. *Collins Easy Learning Dictionary* (Glasgow: HarperCollins Publishers, 2006), p.490

20. Richter, p.71

21. Richter, p.73

22. Richter, p.81

23. Richter, p.87

24. Richter, p.xxvii

25. Collins, p.664

26. Richter, p.121

27. Richter, p.133

28. Richter, p.142

29. Richter, Jean Paul, *Horn of Oberon* (Detroit: Wayne state University Press, 1973), p.lvii

CHAPTER THREE: MISCELLANEOUS WORKS OF JEAN PAUL

Jean Paul had been many things in his time, including poet, novelist, philosopher, scientist and educationalist. He had lived through a turbulent period of history, which had affected the types of work he produced. From bitter satire he developed his Romantic side, being a popular character with many lady friends and seeking his own ideal love, his novels were permeated with romance in all its forms.

Although the *Horn of Oberon: School for Aesthetics,* was not published until 1804, Jean Paul had been preparing his thoughts and theories about the process of creation and the role of the artist, for a number of years. Having begun to formulate his aesthetic questions in 1794, his quest and the completed fragments did not emerge as a whole until 1804. The result was a "delightfully vivid presentation not only of the dominant Romantic idealism but of the more technical conservative counter-currents in aesthetic and literary theory of the time."[1] He had continued to extend his theories with another publication in 1825, followed by the final extension before his death. The theories were compiled as three lectures, or fifteen courses, covering art and aesthetics, literature and criticism, "with a horn of Oberon that can enchant artist and reader, [making it] characteristically Romantic."[2]

Despite the major source of the theories being through the aesthetics of poetry, *Oberon* also commented upon the novel, as well as including a comprehensive examination of humour in all its forms. It seemed relevant, therefore, to begin this chapter with *Horn of Oberon*, and the comments made by Jean Paul about the novel, in order to understand the techniques and style of Jean Paul, and the workings of his mind.

On the novel, Jean Paul stated that it came in two distinctive forms; the dramatic and the epic, and that the most indispensible element in the novel is the Romantic, into whatever form it may be hammered or cast."[3] But it was the epic form of the novel which Jean Paul insisted could contain all the elements of the world, whilst other forms could only show one side of the world. He singled out Goethe's *Meister* as "being true to the epic character, [with a] resurrected spirit of a more Romantic time [which] allows a light, bright, high cloud to pass over which reflects or carries the world and the past, rather than a single hero."[4]

Alongside the Romantic, was a form of the novel that Jean Paul referred to as the idyll, he gave many examples of what he considered to be idyll or idyllic, including his *Maria Wuz* and *Quintus Fixlein*. He commented that it should possess "perfect happiness in limitation,"[5] and that the idyll "requires the brightest local colours not only for the landscape but also for situation, social rank, and character,"[6] discounting the political, referred to as "the power of great wheels of state," and that it was the Lilliputians, the small characters "to whom a garden bed is a forest and who lean against a dwarf tree to gather its fruit."[7] The descriptions echoed his own novels where humble humanity, Romantic nature, and the divine existed in peaceful cooperation, and where the small everyday events can be made joyful or, idyllic.

The section of rules and hints for novelists discussed achieving the perfect conclusion or denouement, in which Jean Paul suggested presenting the problem or dilemma early. It would then be followed by what he termed as 'a means of motivation' before reaching a satisfactory result of lessons learned or a moral to be taught, preferably through a familiar characteristic. He gave the example of *Tom Jones* in which there was the unmasking of an early selfish lie by the hypocritical Blifil.[8] The point being made by Jean Paul was that the problem or conflict should be uncovered "through the necessity of the past, not the needs of the future, but always in the present time."[9] He also indicated that it was important to create the characteristics of the hero first, and that his name had to have some sort of meaning, as it is he the story revolves around. The same principle he applied to his heroines, "every heroine in modern times has, if no other beauty, at least this: an Italian name instead of an Italian face,"[10] developing Jean Paul's aesthetic view of subjective beauty.

Jean Paul insisted that the soul of a character was the important element, around which "everything is created, and which attracts or repels according to its nature."[11] For him that was the initial starting point when creating his characters. According to Jean Paul, the soul of a man could be good, bad, humorous, strong or weak, but that it was in his actions where his true nature would be revealed. The outward appearance of a character he would take from reality, from people encountered and known, and would add new and poetic aspects to their characters. Jean Paul stated that the character should then become alive to the writer so he would know not just the 'how' but the 'why' of what a character may do or not do, seeing him as well as hearing him, so he becomes alive to both reader and writer.

On the strength and weakness of his characters Jean Paul declared that the weaker character could not dominate, only destroy the story, and that a "weak character easily becomes unpoetic and ugly,"[12] whilst the hero "continually reappears in all his works as the fine elemental and universal spirit of his whole being, little changed except in so far as the author himself changes."[13] He claimed the good character must improve and shine morally, whilst the bad character must worsen to emphasise the gap between them. Jean Paul stated that readers would recognise the situation and unconsciously urge the hero to outwit the villain. It was, he claimed, in order to increase the element of love not hate, and that virtue must be rewarded in order to "warm the heart of the last reader."[14] Jean Paul concluded that the formation and development of characters are not worth much without the plot, as is a plot without characters, and that the concentration on a "simple man, meant that drama must maintain the stricter unities of time, place and action, as indeed real life does for us all."[15]

Jean Paul turned to the theme of tragedy and stated that it became a reflection of history, and was governed by a simple character and his life, giving the example of "a frail man whose bite of the forbidden apple may cost him a world."[16] On comedy, he claimed it was down to chance rather than fate, and which [had] no respect for guilt or innocence," instead they [characters] are carried along by the story, rather than by them dominating it. He commented that "the most interesting story is always the most complicated; it is also the slowest, however, and the reader therefore demands it to be more accelerated."[17] Jean Paul suggested that the slow progress of the [epic] novel was just an illusion, and the "most successful and less boring are those writers who stroll at pleasure in their works and who do not find out any sooner than their readers where they will stop and stay."[18]

The aspect of comedy known as the ridiculous was defined by the dictionary as being "very foolish," and the verb to ridicule someone meaning to "make fun of them in an unkind way," whilst the noun described it as "unkind laughter and mockery."[19] Jean Paul stated that the use of the ridiculous could display the wrong means to an end or present and contradict a certain interpretation of the situation, and that "it alone among feelings has a subject matter as inexhaustible as the multitude of crooked lines," and that even the Kantian definition, according to which the ridiculous arises, defined it as "a sudden resolution of expectation into nothingness [with] much to be said against it."[20]

The opposite of the ridiculous was, for the writer, the sublime, allowing for contrasts to be forged between the great and the small. The ridiculous, concluded Jean Paul, "was the infinitely small," but he questioned, "What constituted the ideal smallness?"[21] The comic and the 'folly,' he claimed, were made from smallness, leaving us free to enjoy, laugh and be amused. He went on to provide many examples of the ridiculous, but claimed the distinction would become clearer by investigating the Romantic comic, in order to distinguish between satire, humour, irony and what he termed 'whimsy.'

In contrast to the comic, Jean Paul pointed out that satire often had its roots in an immoral and ugly side. He gave the examples of Young's *Satires* and Pope's *Dunciad*, which contained elements of both the comic and satire, but, he claimed, "the mixture has a moral implication and danger,"[22] and that the English writers fail as they punish folly, when chance and illusion are alone responsible. Jean Paul named Rabelais, Swift and Sterne as the being amongst the great comic writers.

Returning to the ridiculous, Jean Paul concluded that it was "the eternal consequence of spiritual finitude."[23] Margaret Hale commented that his terminology was not easy to understand and called them "verbal cartwheels, [which] are not always enlightening,"[24] as both the ridiculous and the sublime are regarded in terms of 'finitude' and 'infinitude.' She suggested that the terms serve more an emphatic rather than analytical function. From an overall viewpoint it could be implied that the comical illusion of a situation would always remain, depending upon by who, or how it was perceived.

On the element of wit, Jean Paul defined it as being a social power attributed to a person, but that it was also not a faculty which could describe itself. The dictionary defined wit as being "the ability to use words or ideas in an amusing and clever way," and appeared to have its relations with common sense and intelligence, as "they haven't got the wit to know what they are doing," and, "your wits are the ability to think and act quickly in a difficult situation."[25] Friedrich Schlegel had referred to it as "fragmentary genius,"[26] in which the ideal form of the novel would be one without restrictions.

For the writer wit was a useful device for describing dissimilarities and similarities, but also hidden truths through the clever use of wordplay, which alerted the reader to see both sides and uses of a statement, which had also usually been shortened to give a surprise effect on the imagination. Jean Paul pointed out however, that "although the imagination wants to paint, wit [wants] only to colour."[27] Jean Paul was concerned primarily with wit in that aesthetic sense, although he considered wit to be a more mental concept, whilst the ridiculous was purely subjective and human.

Observing the use of wit by other nations, he concluded how "we Germans lack taste, not talent, for wit…in France the whole nation is witty [but] the French cannot produce such witty minds as ours or the British…the Germans and Britons glow more in writing, and risk bolder figures."[28]

Thomas Carlyle had been a great admirer of Jean Paul in England, and had written articles about him, which were published in the *Edinburgh Review* (1827) and *Foreign Review* (1830), as well as translating his works for Carlyle's *German Romance* into English. He stated that "his *Vorschule der Aesthetik* (*Introduction to Aesthetics*) is a work on poetic art, based on principles of no ordinary depth and compass, abounding in novel views, and, not withstanding its frolicsome exuberance, in sound and subtle criticism; esteemed even in Germany, where criticism has long been treated of as a science." On the negative side, Carlyle did point out, as others had done before him, that the *Aesthetics* was not easy to follow or understand, being confusing at times. He did emphasise the phrasing used by Jean Paul of "humour as the inverse sublime –the element of humour, as opposed to the contempt which crops up in so many German versions."[29]

Thomas De Quincey stated that "before 1789 good authors were rare in Germany," and asked, "who is my favourite author?" He gave the answer: both Schiller and Jean Paul. "Schiller," he wrote, "I love his works chiefly because I venerate the memory of the man: whereas, in the case of Richter, my veneration and affection for the man is founded wholly on my knowledge of his works." De Quincey went so far as to claim that Jean Paul was "by far the most eminent artist – since the time of Shakespeare, and that it is to the honour of Jean Paul…he constantly reminds me of Shakespeare. Everywhere a spirit of kindness prevails: his satire is everywhere playful, delicate, and clad in smiles, never bitter, scornful or malignant…Jean Paul's works are the galaxy of the German literary firmament."[30]

The novels written by Jean Paul appeared at regular intervals from 1783 until his death in 1825. Prior to his death he had written the novel *Selena,* and was attempting to complete his autobiography, which he had not begun until 1818, according to George Stuart Collins. The autobiography presented Jean Paul as the "Professor of his own life history, and the three chapters he completed [up to 1776] are called Lectures. These three chapters form the first part of the long biography of Jean Paul by Christian Otto and Ernst Förster... the three lectures which we have, caused great regret that Jean Paul could not have completed his autobiography. No doubt, however, the very circumstances which caused him to relinquish the task, unfinished...might have made the remainder of the work a sharp contrast with the portion completed."[31]

Jean Paul's entrance into the world of literature was, initially, through social satire. Many of his works were in some respects biographical, until experience and maturity led him into the more diverse areas of Romanticism, humour and sentiment. His one consistency was in his philosophy of nature and the universe. Stahl concluded that some of the plots invented by Jean Paul in his novels were, "pointlessly bizarre; in fact, the mistaken or masked identities, cryptic events and sensational revelations often have an ulterior significance – they are emblems of psychological states and crises, spiritual deaths, rejuvenations and resurrections. Alongside – and sometimes embedded within – the tangled intrigues of these stories with their sublime or demonic characters are studies of idyllic contentment in cheerful poverty, or portraits of amiable eccentricity."[32]

Stahl's assessment of the novels gave a multifaceted view of the complexity of scene, the psychology of characters and poetic and Romantic plot, which were invented by Jean Paul. Writing between the eighteenth and nineteenth centuries, meant that influences from both centuries would affect or define the work of a novelist, but Jean Paul's totally unique style made him difficult to categorize. His works included aspects from the sentimental in his past, to the subjective and philosophical questions of his day and the ramifications of writing against the tide of Romanticism, with a large dose of humour to complicate the narrative even more.

Webber also claimed that Jean Paul was "a writer who resists categorical judgements [and that] if he is under-read today it is probably not least because he is a misfit in any literary history. His writing seems to correspond most readily to the Sentimentalist novels of eighteenth –century English literature, the works of such as Sterne or Richardson."[33] But he was writing at the turn of the century, a time when Classicism and Romanticism were established movements. He was also caught up in the philosophical arguments of his day, making his work a combination of idealism, realism, romance, with the philosophical and mystical interwoven. The added use of satire and humour were added to the mix, resulting in a unique narrative product, the equal to any great writer of his day. Jean Paul had discussed his use of humour and how he defined it to his friend Johann Abegg in 1798, as "to find reluctantly the ordinary smallness of human nature while one sublimely hovers midway between pain and elevation above such smallness –to express this is called humour, which offers the appearance of the sublime and of the comic next to one another."[34]

In questioning his own existence, Jean Paul observed everyday humanity, with the mixed emotions of humour and the tragic. His works can be divided into early and later works. The early works of his youth, were enthusiastically written, and often from necessity. In the later works we can appreciate the development and maturity of Jean Paul as a writer and novelist. Although it was through financial need that he wrote his first essays and novels, producing coarse and bitter works of satire, he underwent a transformation following the death of his brother and his friend, which saw a change in his attitude and style.

Further political developments in Germany saw Jean Paul, once again, returning to humour and writing for the people. Satire was the device for which Jean Paul was recognised, alongside the English novelist, Laurence Sterne. Both were equally recognised for their use of digression. Jean Paul had made it his mission to become famous for using more digression than anyone else. It appeared that he was in competition with himself, as his novels illustrated, often making the chronology difficult to follow. Jean Paul had said that his ambition "was to do what no author had ever done: to record for posterity every thought that ever came into his head."[35]

Buckminster Lee also noted how Jean Paul had begun to compile a dictionary, which he added to throughout his life, in which he "wrote down synonyms, and all the shades of meaning of which a word was susceptible. For one word he had found more than two hundred."[36] He was noted for his disregard for form, which made the novels difficult to read, despite his efforts to carefully "sketch the outlines of his characters, the principle scenes, thoughts to be worked in [which he called] *Quarry for Hesperus* or *Quarry for Titan*,"[37] but careful attention to the details revealed the warm and witty nature, the joys and the sorrows of Jean Paul.

Dorothea Berger also raised the issue of digressions and added footnotes, and claimed that Jean Paul employed five different kinds of notes; the first whereby he would give detail and information, to highlight his extensive knowledge; the second, giving hints and illusions that could baffle the reader; the third, which was a running commentary about the action; the fourth translating foreign quotations, "which are sometimes humorous or embarrassing because they destroy the mood of climactic or poetic passages," and the final fifth consisting of aphorisms from his own personal collection.[38]

Jean Paul's linguistic gymnastics may have had his readers shaking their heads with confusion, but the devices he employed allowed him not only to present his story but judge it too. Through such internal speculation Jean Paul could openly display his thoughts and feelings to the readers.

His great love affair with nature, art and music brought the novels to life, making them aesthetic objects. His other works were written because he was a humanitarian, and could not watch the sufferings of his fellow-man and with the inspiration of the French Revolution and take-over of his own homeland, Jean Paul put his writing skills to good use. He produced the *Booklet of Freedom* (1805), demanding freedom of the press, followed by *Sermon on Peace*, and *Twilights for Germany* (1809). Those were just some of the pieces he produced during that part of his life, although he wrote many more articles and essays, an estimated thirteen publications, which helped to support his family during the period of occupation. He continued to write, having many articles published. His later blindness slowed him down, but still did not stop his enterprising spirit. The writing life of Jean Paul had its empathy with the other Romantic writers of the time. His introduction to, and admiration of the Jena group of writers, linked him strongly to their philosophies.

Alongside his novels, Jean Paul wrote shorter stories, which came under the heading of the 'novelle,' which covered pieces of writing, either the short story or similar pieces, such as *Abelard and Heloise* (1781), which was his first love story and was written in the form of letters. The structure and ideas of Goethe's *Werther* had been a source of inspiration for the novel, in its letter form. The story was about his friend Lorenz Adolf von Oerthel and his love for Beata von Spangenberg, the daughter of a neighbour. Dorothy Berger stated that Oerthel's beloved Beata married another man one year after the completion of the novel [and] since Werther wrote letters to a friend, Abelard did the same, also shooting himself to death.[1] The novella was a broad term that had sub-divisions, such as lyrical and epic poetry, and can "presuppose an irrationalistic view of life, and can be fatalistic."[2]

Following his venture into romance writing, Jean Paul developed his skills, including the use of humour. But, his natural talent always took him back to the bigger questions of man, nature, life and death. The question about life after death seemed to haunt most of his serious works.

In *Tales of Humour and Romance*, Holcraft, in his Translators Preface,[3] referred to the 'eccentric' writings of Jean Paul as "perilous ground to tread," and that "one cannot read two sentences of Richter without finding many faults [but that] he never could have acquired so much fame in his own country without some just title to it." Holcraft stated that he found the work of Jean Paul to be "far too sentimental – too imaginative, and too metaphorical, and his characters too simple and unsophisticated for the present state of English readers." He claimed that the reader needed a good deal of imagination; otherwise he recommended that they did not read *Death of an Angel* or *The Moon.* He referred to the translation of a dream by Madame de Stael, "who had made it agreeably to the taste of her countrymen."

Recognising that he had included Jean Paul in his anthology for its 'literary curiosity,' Holcraft apologetically offered that for Jean Paul, he would "show up his merits and demerits, and let the reader judge for himself."

The Moon: A Tale of the Imagination (1796) was one of Jean Paul's first short stories, or novellas, and he stated that it was a "fanciful story."[4] Its initial structure was of a letter to his foster-sister, Philippina, recommending that she should study science and astronomy instead of French romances. The moon was the central image, with the astronomer, Jean Paul making realistic valuations, whilst the poet "furnishes and adorns them." It was a subject which led to Jean Paul's philosophies about man's place in the universe and ultimately, heaven. He indicated that women viewed the moon only in Romantic terms, without considering its function in the constellation. However, at the conclusion of the letter he admitted "it remains a matter of doubt whom I am here addressing, thee or the moon." His admiration for his sister was reinforced by stating that she "resembled the moon in all but its spots and its changeableness."[5]

The narrative moved towards the story itself, which contained the two characters, Rosamond and Eugenius, The setting was an English garden. Jean Paul gave a description of Rosamond as being, 'pierced by sorrow,' and that her husband, Eugenius, possessed a "mighty mind."[6]

The story gave an account of their journey to the mountains, where, it seems, they had gone to die, and a "quiet hut" had been "prepared for therm."[7] Jean Paul gave a beautiful, poetic and mystical account of their arrival on the mountain, between heaven and earth. The illusion was shattered by the death of the child followed by the blindness, and further death, of Eugenius. Rosamond was left alone awaiting death, to which she pleaded, "wherefore can I not die?"[8] It was only through her isolation and grief that she saw the ghosts of Eugenius and the child, to which she learned that she had died.

Jean Paul's melancholy story used the images of the mountains and their proximity to heaven, to illustrate that in later life we are at the half-way point to death. The ever-present theme of death and immortality, and the contrast of the dark earth with the vast, brilliant light of heaven, enfolded the story, with the conclusion that death is not the end but a new beginning, with its "rosy light [which] never departs."[9]

Goethe also, in melancholy style, wrote a poem called *To the Moon*, in which nature reflected the ideal and separate reality of the self. It was a very subjective and highly Romantic poem, evoking the German forest landscape scene, comparing love and loss, life lived and lost. The poem personifies the river with its constant movement both daily and throughout the seasons. Its running movement reflected the ebb and flow of life. Nature was the "trusty friend alone," which would always be there for him to "quietly enjoy."[10]

In the same year as *The Moon*, Jean Paul wrote a similar, but much shorter piece, called *Death of an Angel* (1796)[11] which reflected upon the final hours of approaching death. The angel was the personification of death, who visited in those precious final hours. The story was very mystical and melancholy, with the image of the wounded soldier who awoke to find he was still alive, although in pain. It was a reminder about the transient and short existence of man, but that far from rejecting the idea of death, he embraced it; death being preferable to a life of pain and suffering.

An unexpected poem written by Jean Paul was published in the *Dublin Penny Journal* eight years after his death. It had been submitted under the name of Clarence, although the journal acknowledged that it was the work of Jean Paul. The poem was called *The New-Years-Night of an Unfortunate Man (Die Neujahrsnacht eines Ungluecklichen).*[12] The setting for the poem was, as the poem indicated, New Year's Eve; one year ending and a new one beginning, with reflections upon the past and thoughts about the future.

The poem was structured into eight verses, with rhyming couplets; supernatural and gothic language, the antithesis of the words creating a strong contrast of images; "his dull eyes," "so cold and white," with "groaned," wretchedness and despair, the "worn out frame," the "blighted soul" with "the dark years of agony, remorse, and withering fears."

The Romantic image was of the solitary figure (Jean Paul), whose tragic thoughts and reflections echoed nostalgia for the past, within a supernatural context. With great emotion and remorse the solitary figure had become aware of his own mortality, and he looked back to his childhood where "his father placed him first," making choices for him, but that he had to make his own decisions after that. His thoughts about his father caused him pain and to cry out, "Oh, father" be my guide/And let me only choose my path once more." (26:4)

The images of impending death hovered over the poem, as man, nature, and the changing industrial society were also evoked, and the "huge windmills lifted up their arms to crush/And skeleton faces rose up from the dim/Depths of the charnel-house, and glared on him!" (38-40/5) Music, always so special to Jean Paul, provided the antithesis to the sounds of death, as "Softer emotions o'er him now came stealing." (45/6) providing a calming sensation and return to normality."

The poem had a tragic feel as the figure faced death, taking stock of his life, but recognising that it was God who gave him strength and would guide him to choose the right path in his life, "He wept, and thanked his God that, with the will/He had the power to choose the right path still." (56/7) providing a contrast of the spiritual with the consciousness of his mortality.

The poem was based upon the dream Jean Paul had of his own death, which he recalled in the final verses; "…Still was he young, for he had dreamed the whole." (50/7) Followed by the warning, "This ghastly dream may be thy guide to bliss." (60/8)

The conclusion to the poem acted as a warning about the shortness of life to young people, with an instruction to follow the right path, because, "Vainly thy tears may flow above the urn/Of thy departed youth –it never will return."[63-4/8] It was a stark warning and reality to all, that life passes by so quickly, and in the end we have only memories, and perhaps regrets of what might have been, had we followed a different path.

The poem *A Scene in the Polar Regions* [13] had a similar style and setting to Coleridge's *The Rime of the Ancient Mariner*, with its references to, and personification of the wildness of nature, particularly in regard to the sea which was always seen as vast, hostile, and dangerous.

The South Pole was the objective in Coleridge, where the "ice was here, the ice was there/the ice was all around; it cracked and growled, and roared and howled/like noises in a swound."[14] Jean Paul referred to it as the "silent, iced-walled cloister of the pole… [where he could] "gaze down on the dreary winter of the world." For both, also, the presence of God was central, against the vast landscape of life and nature in which they gained a spacious perspective. The poems represented man as being in "sublime and awful solitude," who could not only reflect on life that has past, but also affirm their continued faith in man's immortality, confirmed by the words of Jean Paul, "I stand/Yet cold and pale on my horizon; soon/ I must go down to the dark realms of ice/But shall I, too, like him, O God, arise/more warm and bright again, to journey through/A long, bright day in they eternity?" Coleridge's conclusion to the supernatural adventures of the mariner, and his alienation from nature, was by returning to the 'real,' and blessing the world around him, "and all together pray/While each to his great Father bends…"

In complete contrast to the sombreness of the poetry, Jean Paul's Jubilate Lectures at Leipzig were full of his usual warmth and humour.

End notes:

1. Berger Dorothy, *Jean Paul Friedrich Richter*, p.20

2. Holcraft, Richard, *Tales of Humour and Romance* (London: Longman, Rees, Orme, Brown and Green, 1829), p.191

3.Holcraft, Preface

4.Holcraft, p.187

5.Holcraft, p.192

6.Holcraft, p.194

7.Holcraft, p.194

8.Holcraft, p.203

9.Holcraft, p.208

10. Goethe, W, in Wadsworth Henry, (Ed.,), *Poems of Places* (http://www.barleby.com/270/8/204.html)

11. Holcraft, Richard, p.177

12. Richter, Jean Paul in *The Dublin Penny Journal* (June, 1833) (http://www.jstor.org/stable/30002801)

13. Richter Jean Paul, in Longfellow, Henry Wadsworth, (Ed.,) *Poems of Places: An Anthology in 31 Volumes* (Boston: James R. Osgood & Co., 1876-79), p.270 (www.bartleby.com/270/)

14. Wright David, ed., *The Penguin Book of English Romantic Verse* (Harmondsworth: Penguin, 1968), p.157

CHAPTER FOUR: JEAN PAUL & HIS CRITICS

Always on the sidelines of his colleagues, and not always known outside of Germany, Jean Paul had made his voice heard, resulting in him gaining critics who were both favourable and fearful. This study aimed to give reviews for both sides, in order to achieve some balance, but found that most critics had only good things to say about Jean Paul.

The German people had some good things to say about Jean Paul, which was reinforced by Henry Wadsworth Longfellow in his book *Hyperion*.[1] The central character, Paul Flemming was the Romantic traveller in Southern Germany, who encountered a German with a lot to say about Jean Paul. Flemming gave his own recollection of Jean Paul (Longfellow), stating that, "in my mind the man and the author are closely united. I never read a page of his writings without seeing his form before me." He went on to describe the appearance of Jean Paul; "there he sits, with his majestic, mountainous forehead, his mild blue eyes, and finely cut nose and mouth; his massive frame clad loosely and carelessly in an old green frock, from the pockets of which the corners of books project, and perhaps the end of a loaf of bread and the nose of a bottle; a straw hat, lined with green, lying near him; a huge walking stick in his hand, and at his feet a white poodle, with pink eyes, and a string round his neck."

From the very graphic description of Jean Paul, the conversation turned to his literary works. The German gentleman stated that the Germans found difficulty understanding Richter, so it must have been very difficult for a foreign reader. Fleming stated that he found that it was the character of the poet which was important, and that "once you understand an author's character, the comprehension of his writings becomes easy."

On Jean Paul's personal qualities as a man, the German claimed that he found them to be tenderness and manliness, "qualities which are seldom found united in so high a degree as in him. Overall he sees, overall he writes, are spread the sunbeams of a cheerful spirit –the light of inexhaustible human love." He continued, "in every man he loves his humanity only, not his superiority. The avowed object of all his literary labours was to raise up again the down-sunken faith in God, Virtue, and Immortality; and in an egotistical, revolutionary age, to warm again our human sympathies, which have now grown cold. And not less boundless is his love for Nature –for this outward, beautiful world. He embraces it all in his arms." It was quite a speech to which Fleming agreed, and responded, "for in his mind all things become idolized. He seems to describe himself when he describes the hero of his Titan…"The German agreed, adding that, "the sword of his spirit had been forged and beaten by poverty. Its temper had been tried by the thirty years' war [which] rather strengthened and sharpened, by the blows it gave and received." He concluded that Jean Paul had made literature his profession; as if he had been divinely commissioned to write…and boasted that he had made as many books as he had lived years."

Fleming asked the German gentleman what he thought were Jean Paul's greatest characteristics, to which he answered, "most undoubtedly his wild imagination and his playfulness [and that] he throws over all things a strange and magic colouring." After giving such a comprehensive and glowing testimonial of the man and his works, he concluded that "Jean Paul was a comet among the bright stars of German literature." He gave an account of how reading Jean Paul's works transported one into another and beautiful world, where, all is a delirious dream of soul and sense." In a more sombre tone, he added that, "as in real life, so in his writings: the serious and the comic, the sublime and the grotesque, the pathetic and the ludicrous, are mingled together."

On a different level, a critic with a more hostile approach was the philosopher Nietzsche, referring to Jean Paul as false, with no sense of humour, but still managed to be a threat to Goethe and Schiller. He stated in 1875, that

"Jean Paul knew a lot, but had no true knowledge; he knew all sorts of tricks in the arts, but had no art, found almost nothing inedible, but had no taste, possessed feeling and seriousness, but when he offered a taste of them, he poured a repulsive broth of tears upon them. Indeed, he had wit – but unfortunately too little for his craving. Hence, he drove his readers to despair precisely through his lack of wit. All in all he was the colourful, strong smelling weed that sprouted up over night on Schiller's and Goethe's fertile fields. He was an easy man, a good man, and yet a curse – a curse in pajamas."[2]

The comments were surprising as Jean Paul had been very popular in Germany during the early nineteenth century. He had usually been the subject of praise not condemnation. However, the comments about him being a weed that had sprouted up over Goethe and Schiller's "fertile fields" proved that Jean Paul had created a lot of interest in his unique works, and was not going to follow the techniques of the rest, but create his own style. He had undoubtedly cast a shadow over the popularity of Goethe, Schiller and others, who had been received him with some suspicion. Nietzsche had found Jean Paul to be a good person but that 'his curse' could cast a long shadow over the future of literature. Perhaps, as Fleming had suggested, Nietzsche may not have read the works correctly or not understood. The works of Jean Paul have always required patience.

Other negative comments included those by Emile Staiger, who commented that, "the man who estranges us from life cannot accompany us through life," and George Lukacs's comment accusing Jean Paul of " petit bourgeoisie reconciliation with the miserable German reality." However, Wolfgang Harich's comments claimed the opposite; that Jean Paul was a "radical revolutionary…his work [being] a confrontation with and denunciation of the German social and political *misère*"[3] Timothy Casey stated that, although the study by Harich was brilliant, it was, in the end, as one-sided as the opposite.

Helen Watanabe O'Kelly claimed that Jean Paul had stayed loyal to the ideals of the Revolution and Enlightenment. [4] His writings of this time, formed in that secularised version of the sermon beloved of Romantic publicists – *Peace-Sermon to Germany*, 1808, *Dawnings for Germany*, 1809, *Perpetual Peace*, 1795, *Phoebus's succession to Mars*, 1814, and the *Political Lentern* sermons, 1810-17 – do not demonise the French occupiers of Germany. Instead they preach moral strength, faith and resistance rather than violent overthrow, emphasising Germany's cultural rather than political power.

Timothy Casey claimed, in conclusion, that Jean Paul was a mixture of the elements people had said about him; he was idyllic or nihilistic, revolutionary or conservative, sentimental or satirical…he represents inwardness for the sake of being one of the main social and political commentators and satirists of his age…all this seems to assume that Jean Paul is a Romantic, which begs many questions."[5]

The Crayon Journal (1856)[6] had published an extensive appraisal of Jean Paul, encouraging its readers, the American public, to "study the writings of this rugged

Thought-hewer," but warning them that "it was no easy work." The author of the article gave a comprehensive glimpse of German mountain life as Jean Paul would have known it, from the beautiful exterior of the surroundings to an interior description of a typical log-cabin. Referring to the people, he claimed they were, "plain and simple…the charm of romance and the poetry of the ancient superstitions are thickly spread over it."

Against that backdrop, he confirmed what many critics before him had stated, that, "the romance of the mountain solitude fired his (Jean Paul's) imagination. The poverty of the family engendered humility of heart, while the sublimity of nature around him fostered loftiness of thought. But his soul, heart and brain were all *home-made*." Of his humour, the author claimed that Jean Paul "gave us a word pregnant with world-wide meaning, which fills us with awe; there a word bristling with gigantic fun, which convulses us with laughter." The admiration continued as he stated that Jean Paul was "one in a million- one in a billion, who connects himself with eternity without feeling lowered by his morality."

The article discussed the importance of women to Jean Paul, and rightly concluded that the respect he had for his mother had provided a platform for his attitude to all the females he met, and wrote about. The article took up that aspect claiming how, "German women did homage to this man as they never did homage before." The author of the article further claimed that "like the artist, who, thoroughly studying one model, builds up in his mind a complete theory of Art, so Jean Paul, by studying thoroughly one woman, built up in his soul a complete knowledge of female character."

The author of the article suggested that as Jean Paul aged and had increased his knowledge, his writings had become more complex, and that "his endeavour to convey all his thoughts to the reader, led him into the error of believing that they must be as intelligible to the reader, as they were to his own understanding. This was the weakness of the man." In attempting to explain his negative thoughts, the author cited other great men of language, such as Carlyle and Emerson, and concluded that "the misfortune of such men is the crushing weight of their knowledge, the disenchanting influence of their experience…so it is with these great word-hewers."

Such words could have had a negative effect upon his attempts to sway the American reading public, but he balanced the negative with the positive affirmation that, with "Jean Paul, at least, the overflowing love of his heart was never clouded by the tortuous reasonings of his brain; but it was this blending of a heart as poetical lover, and of a reason, as prosaical critic, that produced the fatal unintelligibility of his writings, which we cannot help deploring, while we must revere the tender emotions which made it almost a logical necessity."

From the journals of Jean Paul was his own awareness of great men, of whom he claimed, "we have had great spirits, but not great men," but he singled out Rousseau, who "alone is an exception. His talents made him great as an individual; his heart allied him to all humanity. We love him the more because he discovered his faults to us, and was not ashamed to be our fellow creature." Rousseau had been one of the main people who had influenced Jean Paul throughout his life, from the initial taking of his name to the adopting of ideas inspired by Rousseau. The article discussed the educational philosophy of Jean Paul in his *Levana,* and that "no writer upon education has thrown so much light upon the holy and hidden impulses of a child's soul; no one has written with such reverence of the childish nature, and the necessity in a teacher to respect the individuality of the child." Again, the influence of

Rousseau can be identified, with certain aspects having more than a passing reflection and resemblance of ideas.

The article continued to discuss the life of Jean Paul, highlighting certain incidents, from his relationship with the Herder's to that of royalty, and to his meeting with Caroline Meyer, to the birth of his children. Finally, the article paid tribute to Eliza Buckminster Lee, who had written extensively about the life of Jean Paul, and who had provided the reading public with an excellent translation and biography so useful to all scholars and readers alike.

In a later article published in *The Crayon* (1859)[7] C.T. Brooks questioned why Jean Paul had not reached the same height of fame as Goethe and Schiller, and examined some of the reasons for that. Jean Paul's life had spanned both the eighteenth and early nineteenth centuries, and as Brook pointed out, "that in Jean Paul many characteristics of that revolutionary period reached over into the nineteenth century...the writings of this man belonged to a class which was then cherished and afterwards forgotten."

Brooks discussed how the education of Jean Paul at Leipzig had been cut short due to the death of his father, and his mother's subsequent poverty. However, as he stated, the taste for learning and reading other authors had made its mark, and it seemed the only natural course for him was to become an author. Brooks pointed out how Jean Paul put "his own personality so entirely into the foreground, and sympathy for his stories and characters into the background."

Differentiating between the lifestyles of Goethe and Schiller with Jean Paul, Brooks pointed out that Jean Paul, born in the countryside, had not had any of the luxuries that Goethe and Schiller were accustomed to, so the themes Jean Paul wrote about were truthful in that they represented the life he knew.

Jean Paul confessed about the subjective stance of his works, that he had "no capacity to be a biographer proper." Brooks claimed that Jean Paul, despite his protestations, had taken his influences from his past, in which "all strands isolated, strung on a thread, without necessary order or any object," and referred to him as a historian.

When discussing the critical appreciation of Jean Paul, Brooks referred to how Jean Paul had "always complained of the want of apt critics and judges of his works... he had found only determined praisers or blamers –that his coldest readers held him incapable of improvement, his warmest as not needing any." Brooks suggested that the best critic of Jean Paul "will be he who has once been enthusiastic with him and then grown cool; who has heard the greatest number of chords which his writings can touch vibrate within him, and can give himself an account of his good qualities, without being blind to his bad ones," but as Brooks pointed out, "to hold a middle course with a writer who himself held none, is almost impossible."

Brooks looked upon the idyllic mountain retreat and life of Jean Paul, attempting to find some classification for his works, which proved difficult as "he heard now no lectures, read no books, but such as answered his immediate purposes [but that he]devoted the first, heartiest diligence of the age which lays the groundwork for further culture...not to that of finding for the yet pliable spirit, by comparison and trial, a suitable direction...he looked back to nothing more enchanting than the inner life of that period," suggesting that Jean Paul was happy to be part of the great enlightenment, with its period of Romantic introspective thought. Brooks claimed that all the works of Jean Paul were full of youthfulness from that period, "like a man who remains forever young," and like the poet, the reader is lifted "far above common life." It seemed odd that in contrast with that image, Brooks reminded how Jean

Paul's collecting of reflections and devotions made him obey "every strict demand of reason." As with all his works, Jean Paul uses many facets of his imagination which make it difficult at times to pin down his direction, but faith, spirituality and the destiny of man are all strong elements, which give more weight to the theory of his links with Romanticism. The elements of reason appear unexpectedly through the use of wit, and the digressions that are very grounding.

Although the article by Brooks had initially praised Jean Paul, its focus also fell onto the negative aspects with that attempt to find some balance, which he had previously declared was not easy. However, Brooks claimed that Jean Paul had missed one thing; a classical education. As Brooks stated, Jean Paul had indeed rejected the ancient Greeks, and that it was the reason why there was such a contrast between him, and opposition to, Goethe and Schiller. Brooks saw Jean Paul as a modern Romantic of the time, "especially when he is joined by Fouque and Hoffmann." Brooks also criticised Jean Paul's attempts at satire, and that it was his "limited knowledge, triviality of the subjects and oddity of style that made them insignificant." The comments appear to be an odd appraisal, as the satires were popular with the German reading public during the Jena war. However, Brooks would have been referring to Jean Paul's first efforts into satire which were written early on, and which failed to be published. It was then that he diverted his talents into a more Romantic framework.

The one truth that emerged from the examination by Brooks, was that Jean Paul was an original. The digressions, he claimed, were of "an extraordinary and extravagant manner," which ran parallel with the use of 'Romantic ingredients' in his novels, which all combined to make him "an original himself."

Thomas Carlyle[8] had been the instrument heralding the arrival of Jean Paul's works into England, in the early eighteen twenties. He gave a full comprehensive appraisal of the writings in his own works, which comprised of thirty volumes. The second volume: The *German Romantics*, was where Jean Paul, alongside Hoffmann and Tieck, was located. In order to persuade the English reading public, Carlyle admitted the difficulty of the task because of the eccentric style, and being full of the 'peculiarities' adopted by Jean Paul. After reference to the "theatrical clap-traps and literary quackery," he concluded by acknowledging that all the elements in the novels, with their "wit, knowledge and imagination, were the work of a glorious intellect."

Carlyle continued to comment on the style and structure of the works, which "groaned with indescribable metaphors and allusions to all things human and divine, stating that there are some "wild digressions upon any subjects but the one in hand," leaving the reader exhausted with mixed feelings of astonishment, oppression and perplexity." He concluded that "Richter stands before us in brilliant cloudy vagueness, a giant mass of intellect but without form, beauty or intelligible purpose."[9]

From the initial confusion and criticism, Carlyle admitted that the novels did have a "meaning, and often a true and deep one," and that all the elements of his structure are vast, and "combined together in living and life-giving, rather than in beautiful or symmetrical order."[10]

With reference to the humour of Jean Paul, Carlyle said, "he can play at bowls with the sun and moon [and that] his imagination "opened for us the Land of Dreams [as] we sail with him through the boundless abyss, and the secrets of Space, Time, and Life."[11] with regard to Jean Paul's imaginative processes, Carlyle highlighted the "mysterious allegories, visions and typical adumbrations [and that] his Dreams, in particular, have a gloomy vastness…shadowy forms of meaning rise dimly from the bosom of the void Infinite."[12]

But it was the humour of his writings which had most impressed Carlyle, and which he found to be his 'ruling quality, and how "in this rare gift- for none is rarer than true humour – he stands unrivalled in his own country; and among late writers, in every other."[13] Carlyle described the humour of Jean Paul as "vast, rude, irregular; often perhaps overstrained and extravagant; yet fundamentally it is genuine humour, the humour of Cervantes and Sterne, the product not of Contempt but of Love, not of superficial distortion of natural forms, but of deep though playful symphony with all forms of Nature."[14] He remarked about the type of humour often used by Jean Paul, and how he would throw some slight incident before us and how we would "smile at it perhaps, but with a smile more sad than tears," but it was on the strength of the accompanying endowments, Carlyle concluded, that Jean Paul's main success as an artist depended.[15]

Turning to the characters created by Jean Paul in his novels, Carlyle stated how they would always "have a dash of the ridiculous in their circumstances, or their composition, perhaps in both," but with the feeling that Jean Paul was laughing "no less than we at their ineptitudes. He singled out the characters of Fixlein, Siebenkas, Fibel and Schmelzle, commenting that they "had found a place closer to our hearts than that of many more splendid heroes."[16]

Carlyle commented that the elements which combined to create such humour was "a test of true humour; no wit, no sarcasm, no knowledge will suffice; not talent but genius will accomplish the result." Carlyle suggested that as long as the humour was present, Jean Paul would continue to "create higher and stronger characters."[17]

For the heroes, however, Carlyle stated that they were more problematic, and "in some instances they verge towards absolute failure…they call themselves Men, and do their utmost to prove the assertion, but they cannot make us believe it." He suggested that Jean Paul's heroes do not usually assume the air of truth"[18] and are propped up with the usual adornments of wit, knowledge, fancy and imagination, to create an artistic and delightful picture.

On a more personal level, Carlyle found Jean Paul to be a man with "a mild, humane, beneficient spirit which breathes through his works."[19] Nature, in particular was the passion of Jean Paul and to which all critics could not overlook. Carlyle pointed out Jean Paul's descriptions, "from the solemn phases of the starry heaven to the simple floweret of the meadow, [with] his eye and his heart...open for her charms and her mystic meanings."[20] Nature was the inspiration for Jean Paul to create, invent, and find peace. His greatest thoughts were conceived when lying under the open sky, and which later found their way into whatever piece he was working on at that time, or recorded and systematically saved to pull out when the need arose.

Having been brought up as the son of a clergyman Jean Paul's soul had been touched by religion, as well as the subject of immortality. It was a theme that occurred time and again in his novels, and as Carlyle commented, "in Richter alone, among the great (and even sometimes truly moral) writers of his day, do we find the Immortality of the Soul, expressly insisted on, nay, so much incidentally alluded to."[21]

In conclusion, Carlyle again repeated, how difficult the works of Jean Paul were for the English readers, and that only through long and sedulous study can any meaning be found. He suggested that such study would help the reader to pass from confusion and "half contemptuous wonder" to "reverence and love."[22]

The North American Review, (1863), published a comprehensive article about the life and works of Jean Paul. Taking one of the main themes; nature, the reviewer stated that Jean Paul's "enjoyment of natural scenery and phenomena was pervasive [amounting to] an intense passion,"[23] and that "he walked hand in hand with the seasons, communed with forest and mountain, sky and river…a sublime landscape or a lovely sunset would thrill him with rapture, melt him to tears, make him turn pale and tremble…his sensibility was world-embracing, world-dissolving. He had withal an Oriental vastness of imagination, which could suffuse the universe with its own colour and feeling, animate the very spaces of infinitude, and set the wilderness of astronomic orbs in motion."[24]

From the exterior nature he turned to Jean Paul's caring and emotional concern for humanity, concurring that he had "mind to reproduce and heart to cherish everything that concerns human nature…indeed, the mighty exuberance of pure and generous emotion, the ocean of tenderness, exposed in the writings of Jean Paul, we know of no author in all the circuits of literature who can rival."[25]

The critic pointed out the opposite side to Jean Paul's personality, seeing freedom as the right of every individual, an issue of which he spoke out strongly. He referred to the article written by Jean Paul called *Freedom's Pamphlet,* in which he protested against a princely or state censorship of the press, and to the words of Jean Paul, "Only weak, caterpillar-and-hedgehog-like souls curl and crumple up into themselves at every touch; under the free brain beats gladly a free heart."[26]

As stated in the title of this study, Jean Paul's personality was, like his writings, multifaceted. The critic also referred to that fact, confirming how Jean Paul had a "special fellow-feeling and a soothing pity for the poor, oppressed, broken-hearted,- for all sufferers; and he [had] also special hyperborean, biting frosts and stings for the haughty and luxurious, for all pompous pretenders, all cruel tyrants." His novels dealt effectively, although not cruelly, with characters who displayed such qualities. There was always the lesson to be learned through the pen of Jean Paul.

The sentimental side of Jean Paul was visible when children became the subject, and most of his writings included reference to them in one form or another. At times he appeared to grieve for his childhood, and at others he displayed child-like qualities in his personality. As father to three children he would have noted all the habits; both good and bad, their virtues and vices, and when it came to educating them none was more capable than Jean Paul. His teaching and educational methods found their way into his Levana, which proved to be hugely popular. The critic of the article cited Jean Paul's words from *Flower, Fruit and Thorn Pieces*, about children, "Ah, were I only for a little time almighty, I would create a world especially for myself, and suspend it under the mildest sun; a little world where I would have nothing but lovely little children; and these little creatures I would never suffer to grow up, but only to play eternally."[27]

Despite the derogatory, although applied with wit remarks, made in his novels about the subject of women, the critic called Jean Paul the earnest friend and student of woman." He continued that "woman has never had among literary men a more staunch or a more judicious defender, counsellor, and eulogist than Jean Paul...they cannot read him without throbbing hearts in many passages, streaming tears in many others, valuable instruction and elevating impulse in nearly all."[28]

To illustrate his point, he referred to the *Extra Leaf* in the *Titan*, which had for its title, *The Green Market of Daughters*, and contained a "terrible satire on mercenary marriages negotiated by parents, whose caustic irony is only less than its tragic pathos and truth of thought and fact" He concluded, "women can conceal nothing from Jean Paul."[29] Jean Paul was a good judge of women and his insights into the different personalities was quite fascinating. He had been very popular with the ladies, but had always been trying to find his 'ideal' woman, without success, for many years. He had been acquainted with many women of different rank and stature, and that would have been a valuable lesson for him, in observation.

The most distinctive trait of Jean Paul for the reviewer was in his serious earnestness and overpowering pathos, with imaginative humour and comicality, and that "he is as much at home in the sublime as in the ridiculous…he is three-headed, three-hearted giant, equipped with an equal perception of the droll and the dread."[30] He singled out those opposites in the characters of Ottoman and Fenk in the *Invisible Lodge*, Siebenkas and Leibgeber in *Fruit, Flower and Thorn Pieces*, Victor and Emanuel from *Hesperus*, from *Titan*; Albano and Schoppe, and finally the two brothers, *Walt and Vult.* Those characters worked at opposite poles, like doppelgangers, or mirror images, but with their own personalities, allowing Jean Paul to alternate his own thoughts, feelings, and opinions.

As other critics have stated previously about Jean Paul's "bewildering array of incidental material, it again re-surfaced in this article, with the critic commenting upon Jean Paul's "sporadic mind and style [which] bewilder and weary the reader, who has not agile faculties and wealthy resources to follow his clues of swift and complex allusion," but he did concede that "a dish of pearls may be costly and beautiful, though neither strung nor arranged."[31]

In a more recent article published in the *North Wind* (*Journal of the George MacDonald Society*), in 1995[32] William Webb examined the relationship between the ideologies of George Macdonald and Jean Paul. George MacDonald was a Scottish mid-Victorian writer, author of *Alec Forbes of Howglen*[33] and *A Dish of Orts*[34] plus many more. Webb pointed out the influences Jean Paul had inherited from Sterne, with the "sudden changes of mood [and] strange digressions, and his fondness for learned footnotes, with imagery and illusions…often derived from extraordinary items in encyclopaedias of the time." Sterne, according to Webb, was the only author for whom MacDonald "had an active dislike, and in his novel, *Alex Forbes*, his character Mr Cupples maintains that Sterne's Tristram Shandy is "a pailace o' dirt and impidence and speeritual stink!"

Webb called Jean Paul's use of the dream technique very 'original,' which could be sometimes "mysterious and apocalyptic, and [could] even express a tragic nihilism." A particular dream sequence referred to by Webb that had impressed MacDonald, was that of the dead Christ from *Flower, Fruit & Thorn Pieces*. It was images such as these which inspired MacDonald to use them in his own novels. Webb cited the novel Wilfred Cumbermede, which has a dark and pessimistic tone, and a love affair that ends in frustration. But it was the dream sequences that were, according to Webber, "unusually macabre."

Webb cited themes such as mirror images, doppelgangers and duplicate selves which had a great appeal to writers of fantasy such as Hoffmann and Tieck, and that they were also present in MacDonald's *Phantastes*, the *Flight of the Shadow* and *Lilith*.

With reference to Titan by Jean Paul, Webb used the character of Schoppe to illustrate a point: Schoppe attended a fancy-dress ball carrying a glass case in which figures imitated the dancing humans, and were then reflected in a mirror at the back. He compared the incident to George Macdonald's in *A Dish of Orts*, in which he" felt himself involved in a similar situation of multiple reflections."

Webb suggested that Jean Paul may have been influenced by Novalis (1772-1804), with his similar ideas, thoughts and approach to mysticism and transcendentalism.

Although Webb had attempted to forge a connection between George MacDonald and Jean Paul, the evidence was very tentative, although it seemed likely that there had been a lot of admiration for Jean Paul by MacDonald, who had subsequently adopted some of the techniques for his own works. The novels he produced were quite different to those of Jean Paul, often taken from fairy tales or relying upon "imaginative theology and symbolic fantasy." He had received the admiration of C.S.Lewis, who stated, "I have never concealed the fact that I regarded him as a master; indeed I fancy I have never written a book in which I did not quote from him." Webb's final comments to his brief article were, however, very positive, as he pointed to the words of Sherlock Holmes (an unlikely coupling), "from the novel *The Sign of Four*, chapter seven; "there is much food for thought in Richter."

Giles P.Hawley had compiled a book called *Wit, Wisdom and Philosophy of Jean Paul Friedrich Richter*[35] Its provocative title suggested a good critical appraisal, but instead he had compiled samples from the works of Richter and placed them in respective sections; nature, friendship, love; society, and what he termed "gems of thought and brilliant analects."[36] The idea was to allow the American reading public an opportunity to learn about the thoughts, beliefs, style of Richter without actually having to read the books. He claimed, "the compiler of this volume believes that there are many well-informed people who cannot find time for the laborious task of reading this voluminous author."[37]

There have been many such reviews as these written during the nineteenth century, all full of praise for Jean Paul his caring and compassionate nature, his insights into the minds and worlds of men. After a full and fitting oration, the author Ludwig Börné completed his article in *The Crayon*, 1860, with the following closing words, summing up the life of Jean Paul,

"No hero, no poet, has indicated such true information about his life as Jean Paul has done. The spirit has fled, the word remains! He has gone back to his home; and in whatever heaven he may be wandering, on whatever star he may dwell, he will never in his glorification forget his familiar earth, nor his dear fellow-men, who played and wept with him, and loved and endured as did he."[38]

Wilkinson, too, at the end of his essay had summed up the life and death of Jean Paul, stating, "they buried him by torchlight, the manuscript of his last work, still unfinished – a tractate on the immortality of the soul – borne, a symbol on his coffin. But the tears of a nation that loved the man as well as the author, made an amber to embalm him for immortality. There had ceased a German such as never was before, such as never would be after. It was Jean Paul the Only."[39]

1. Longfellow, Henry Wadsworth, *Hyperion* (Boston: James R. Osgood & Company, 1871), p.31-43

2. Fleming Paul, *The Pleasures of Abandonment: Jean Paul and the Life of Humour* (Bonn/New York: Konigshausen & Neumann, 2006), p.89

3. Casey Timothy, F, *Jean Paul: A Reader* (Baltimore & London: John Hopkins University, 1992), p.4

4. O'Kelly Helen Watanabe, *Cambridge History of German Literature* (Cambridge: Cambridge University Press, 2000), p.257

5. Casey, p.5

6. The Crayon, volume 3, No: 12, Dec., 1856, p.356-361 (http://www.jstor.org/stable/25527882)

7. Brooks, T.C, *The Crayon,* vol: 6, No: 4 (April, 1859), p.101-109 (http://www.jstor.org/stable/25527882

8. Carlyle Thomas, *German Romance: Translations from the German with Biographical and Critical Notes*. (London: Chapman & Hall Limited, 1827), p.117

9. Carlyle, p.118

10. Carlyle, p.119

11. Carlyle, p.120

12. Carlyle, p.120

13. Carlyle, p.120

14. Carlyle, p.121

15. Carlyle, p.121

16. Carlyle, p.121

17. Carlyle, p.122

18. Carlyle, p.122

19. Carlyle, 123

20. Carlyle, p.123

21. Carlyle, p.124

22. Carlyle, p.125

23. North American Review, Vol: 97, No.200 (July, .1863):

(http://www.jstor.org/stable/25100382), p.6

24. North American, p.7

25. ibid, p.8

26. ibid, p.9

27. ibid, p.12

28. ibid, p.12

29. ibid, p.12

30. ibid, p.14

31. ibid, p.16

32.Webb William, *The North Wind Journal of the George MacDonald Society*, p.2

(http://www.ev90481.dial.pipex.com/gmsociety/nw14_jeanpaul.htm)

33. MacDonald George, *Alec Forbes of Howglen* (London: Hurst & Blackett, 1867)

34. MacDonald George, *A Dish of Orts* (London: Sampson Low Marston & Co, 1895)

35. Hawley Giles, *Wit, Wisdom & Philosophy of Jean Paul Friedrich Richter* (New York: Funk & Wagnalla, 1884), preface.

36. Hawley, preface

37. Hawley, preface

38. Börné Ludwig, The Crayon, Vol: 7, No.11 (November, 1860), p.305

(http://www.jstor.org/stable/25528132)

39. Wilkinson William Cleaver, *Classic German Course in English* (New York: Chautauqua Press, 1891), p.139

CHAPTER FIVE: CONCLUSION – Romantic or Realist?

The weight of evidence for placing Jean Paul in the category of Romanticist or Realist had to be itemised and defined for its literary art, as well as its point in history. Whilst it became clear that his style was very much that of the Romanticist, in the areas of music, philosophy and religion there was also that of the realist, where digression full of information, often with irony, wit and humour, became integral parts of the work. Paul Fleming identified the authors Holderlin and Kleist, writing in the same era as Jean Paul, as writers who also defied classification," and referred to Jean Paul as a unique literary voice."[1]

Helen Watanabe-O'Kelly in the *Cambridge History of German Literature* also attempted to classify Jean Paul, stating that, as has been found, that his work "embodies bewildering polarities, from enraptured religious ecstasy to cold nihilism, from satirical distance to emotional dissolution, from sober realism to pure aesthetic play. The common denominator of this he shared, however, with all writers of the age which could be explained as consciousness of division."[2]

Those comments seemed to cover much of the overall appearances of the works, which were often complex and full of eccentricities. But when considering how Jean Paul's works were all embroidered with the consistency and worship of nature, combined with death and the immortality of the soul, the argument ceases; he was a true Romantic, that is, if we rely upon visual appearances and accept a certain type of definition. A 'type' of definition can only be suggested, as there were many types of Romanticism, countries, poets and writers who all wanted to be a part of the Romantic movement, but who approached it with individual ingredients.

Romanticism itself had always been difficult to define exactly, with only the typical and visual characteristics to help with the quest. Burgum commented with great insight that, "he who seeks to define Romanticism is entering a hazardous occupation which has claimed many victims."[3]

It would be true to state, however, that the Romantic writers reached out to much wider audiences, and had greater success than their predecessors. In that sense they were responsible for their influencing effects upon society and its culture.

Bernbaum quoted from many different literary sources what the term Romanticism meant. The results were quite startling as they were all different, and in the end not one had come to a satisfactory conclusion. What they did show was how wide-ranging Romanticism was, and that all writers classed as Romantics still had their own individual styles, despite having the common elements we recognised as Romanticism. Bernbaum confirmed this in his further comments, "those who have studied the leading Romantics will have observed that there is much similarity among their views despite surface differences, and that their attitudes to God, Man and Nature are essentially in harmony, as well as their principles of art and literature."[4]

He stressed how the Romantics were "keenly conscious of the difference between two worlds; one being the world of truth, goodness and beauty this was eternal, infinite, and absolutely real. The other was the world of actual appearances, which to common sense was the only world, and which to the idealist was so obviously full of untruth, ignorance, evil, ugliness, and wretchedness, as to compel him to dejection or indignation."[5]

Bernbaum saw that as Romanticism grew and developed, the Romantics became aware that the ideal world and the real world were not so isolated from each other. However, as Bernbaum pointed out, the anti-Romantics, New Critics and Humanists claimed that science had made it impossible to maintain Romantic beliefs about Nature and Man. The scientific universe meant that art, literature and religion were "merely pleasant narcotics enabling him to escape from the brutal facts into false dreaming."[6]

However much impact the reality of science had made it could not prevent "freedom, reason, imagination and love", which was reinforced by the statement of W.Macneile Dixon in the book *The Human Situation*; "By her own methods nature has brought us into being…by her own methods she has elevated us to intellectual heights whence other heights can be discerned…Man [and] his range of vision; his lonely passion for ideas and ideals far removed from his material surroundings and animal activities…he will stand until he dies, the profound conviction he entertains being that if nothing be worth dying for nothing is worth living for."[7]

The key to the conundrum appeared to be in man's intellect, and that the imagination was a gift of nature, which should not be ignored. Jean Paul had been helpful, in that in his work there was much that was considered Romantic; the spiritual and religious, coupled with a deep love of nature. Heine commented about the literary position of Jean Paul, and that he "appeared at almost the same time as the Romantic school without in the least taking part in it, just as he later felt not the least bit of commonality with Goethe's artistic direction. He stands entirely alone in his

- 157 -

age, precisely because he- unlike the other two schools of thought-gave himself entirely to his age and his heart was entirely filled by it. His heart and his writings were one and the same." Fleming stated that Jean Paul did indeed write *for* his age, in comparison with Goethe and Schiller who wrote for future generations, thus, "the Age of Goethe should have been the Age of Jean Paul."[8]

Karl Ameriks also agreed that Jean Paul was very much involved in the cultural revolution, and stated that, "an unprecedented cultural revolution was taking place...and the arrival of the new and –at least for a while – radically non-conformist generation rich with aesthetic and scientific talent. In addition to those already named, its leading figures were Friedrich Heinrich Jacobi, Freidrich Schleiermacher, Ludwig Tieck, Jean Paul Richter, August Wilhelm Schlegel, Dorothea Schlegel, Caroline Schlegel, and Wilhelm and Alexander von Humboldt."[9]

The historical period that Jean Paul was writing in could not fail to have had some meaning for him, and freedom of the spirit remained his goal, as "civil commotions, wars and revolutions, which shook kingdoms to their foundations, overturned monarchies, and freed nations had been groaning under despotism for hundreds of years."[10] Romanticism when viewed as a historical movement, was connected to the Industrial Revolution in England, the political in France and the social and economic in Russia, effecting far-reaching consequences throughout Europe. Jean Paul did not remain untouched by those events.

His own religious background, his thirst for education, and quest for knowledge about the world around him, fed his philosophical outlook, and eventual works. Armed with that knowledge the reader would expect his novels to be factual and realistic. However, the imagination of Jean Paul conjured up visions of mountains, flowers and trees, woodlands and streams, starry skies and exotic islands and the whole landscape of life, whilst questioning infinity and the immortality of the soul. His fictional characters displayed depth and sensitivity, whilst moods would be transmitted through the music of horns and flutes. His music was an ever-present characteristic representing the Romantic and spiritual.

The novel had taken on a whole new form under the pen of Jean Paul, "riddled with postponed prefaces, multiple appendices, repeated interruptions, an omniscient narrator named Jean Paul [with] satirical extra pages, fields of metaphors, and mounds of footnotes." His narratives were complex, difficult and original, no wonder he claimed, with humour, that he had to "append a book to every preface I write." Fleming,[11]

In the whole area of literature it has been difficult to find another writer who was like Jean Paul. Critics have pointed to Sterne, who could compete with humour and digression. But not for depth of vision and spirituality, which causes the problems of where to place Jean Paul. His unique and original style placed him in a class of his own. He had an intellectual appetite which saw him questioning and commenting with an active and vast imagination, through character, plot and setting. But, the comment made by Friedrich Schlegel that Jean Paul was "the only Romantic writer in an unRomantic age,"[12] before Jean Paul himself was ready to acknowledge his loyalty to the Romantics, answered the important question. As a friend and colleague of Jean Paul, he was at the centre of the Jena group and shared many of the ideas put forward by him, particularly the theories of humour. Jean Paul's *Horn of Oberon*, with its theories and ideas about the current state of literature, was again a Jean Paul original developed into an almost complete and comprehensive guide to Romanticism.

"In literature, every man, said Lessing, has his own style, like his own nose;" Maurice Cross interpreted that to mean "the outward style is to be judged by the inward qualities of the spirit which it is employed to body forth; that without prejudice to critical propriety, well understood, the former may vary into many shapes as the latter varies; that in short, the grand point for a writer, is not to be of this or that external make and fashion, but in every fashion to be genuine…for Richter knows his aims and pursues them in sincerity of heart, joyfully and with undivided will. A harmonious development of being, the first and last object of all true culture, has therefore been attained; if not completely, at least more completely than in one of a thousand men."[13]

The influences from neighbouring countries, the struggles and the visions of great writers and poets and their individual imaginations, their fight against oppression of mankind in its various forms, transformed an entire continent. The resulting emotional and spontaneous outpourings in the world of literature changed forever how man perceived himself, whilst the questions thrown up by the Romantic writers were considered by the philosophers, as questions which could only be answered by a realistic, or scientific approach.

Many authors had chosen to record the features of ordinary life in a bid to leave a documentary of history and incorporated many of the narrative, dramatic, moral or theological styles into their novels.

According to Isaiah Berlin, Romanticism left a legacy, or rather its consequences, in the form of existentialism, "the truest heir of Romanticism," in France, in the way that it changed certain values. The sincerity of ideals, with "sincerity becoming a virtue in itself [and] was at the heart of the whole thing" He pointed to Romanticism undermining "the notion that in matters of value, politics, morals, aesthetics there are such things as objective criteria which operate between human beings...the division between where objective truth obtains – in mathematics, in physics, in certain regions of common sense – and where objective truth has been compromised – in ethics, in aesthetics and the rest – is new, and has created a new attitude to life – whether good or bad...[14]

Berlin's final conclusion was that Romanticism had produced "liberalism, toleration, decency and an appreciation of the imperfections of life; some degree of increased rational self-understanding [and were] the persons who most strongly emphasised the unpredictability of all human activities...they produced, fortunately for us all, almost the exact opposite," fuelling the fire for further debate. In looking to the future, Berlin admitted that Romanticism was not just historical, claiming that "a great many phenomena of the present day –nationalism, existentialism, admiration for great men, admiration for impersonal institutions, democracy, totalitarianism – are profoundly affected by the rise of Romanticism, which enters them all. For this reason it is a subject not altogether irrelevant even to our own day."[15]

Finally, Jean Paul was witness to all the great changes taking place in the late eighteenth and early nineteenth centuries, and indeed was very much a part of promoting them. Having been privileged to be part of an influential group of philosophers, poets and writers, he had carved out his own approach, in an original, creative and spiritual way, that led to great success and popularity in Germany, and only afterwards in a more global way. His readers and students of literature had at last recognised the true genius of the man.

As originality and freedom of creativity came to be recognised as integral parts of Romanticism; the originality and mirroring of the soul, the subjective verses the objective, the spiritual rather than the material, the humour of small things, all of those occupied the imagination of Jean Paul. His *Horn of Oberon* gave further evidence of his attachment to Romanticism. Finally, despite the humour and realistic thoughts he brought to his work, Jean Paul's imagination and novels were overall examples emerging from his underlying, creative Romanticism. They were elements that made him unique in his time. But, without attempting to force him into any type of category, it would be appropriate to consider his character and that of his works, within the historical time frame. He embraced the Romantic, but also remained true to his own nature; full of the spirit of humanity, questioning his own destiny and faith, whilst having an overwhelming appreciation for the aesthetic beauty of nature.

Arthur O. Lovejoy pointed out, in his *Need to Distinguish Romanticisms*, that "the interpretation of the Romantic ideal suggested that the first and greatest commandment is: Be yourself, which is to say, be unique!"[16]

Jean Paul was recognised as being unique, a fact which this study had also uncovered, therefore, it would seem in conclusion, that all students and critics of the author and his works would be correct, in this instance, to finally confer the title of **Romantic** upon Jean Paul. He, no doubt, would have been very pleased with this assessment.

End Notes:

1. Fleming Paul, *The Pleasures of Abandonment* (Bonne: Konighausen & Neumann, 2006), p,12

2. O'Kelly, Watanabe, Helen, (ed.) *The Cambridge History of German Literature* (Cambridge: Cambridge University Press, 2000), p.242

3. Gleckner Robert, F. *Romanticism: Points of View* (Englewood Cliffs, NJ: Prentice Hall, 1962), p.144

4. Gleckner, p.90

5. Gleckner, p.91

6. Gleckner, p.92

7. Gleckner, p.95

8. Fleming, p.12-13

9. Ameriks Karl, *The Cambridge Companion to German Idealism* (Cambridge: Cambridge University Press, 2000), p.2

10. 1. Richter, Jean Paul F, *Sketches of and from Jean Paul* (Oxford: A.W. Bennett, 1859), p.4

11. Fleming, p.17

12. Richter, Horn of Oberon, p.xliii

13. Cross Maurice, *Selections from the Edinburgh Review, vol: 2* (France, Paris: Baudry's European Library, 1835), p.456

14. Berlin Isaiah, *The Roots of Romanticism* (U.S.A: Princeton University Press, 1999), p.162

15. Berlin, p.xxii

16. Lovejoy O. Arthur in Halsted John, B, *Romanticism: Definition, Explanation, and Evaluation* (Boston: D.C Heath & Company, 1965), p.43

BIBLIOGRAPHY

Primary Sources: **Jean Paul**

Lee, Buckminster Eliza, *Life of Jean Paul Freidric Richter*, volume 1(U.S.A, Boston: Charles C Little & Jams Brown, 1842)

Lee. Buckminster Eliza, *Life of Jean Paul Freidric Richter,* volume 2 (London: John Chapman, 1845)

Richter, Jean Paul, *Maria Wutz & Lorenz Stark* (U.S.A, Memphis: General Books LLC, 2012)

Richter, Jean Paul, *The Invisible Lodge* (New York: Henry Holt & co, 1883)

Richter, Jean Paul, *Hesperus or Forty-Five Dog Post Days* (U.S.A, Boston: Ticknor & Fields, 1864)

Richter, Jean Paul, *The Campana Thal* (London: Charles Gilpin, 1848)

Richter, Jean Paul, *Flower Fruit & Thorn Pieces* (Leipzig: Bernhard Tauchnitz, 1871)

Richter, Jean Paul, *Titan* (Cambridge: Welch, Bigelow, And Company, 1862)

Richter, Jean Paul, *Horn of Oberon* (Detroit: Wayne State University Press, 1973)

Richter, Jean Paul, *Levana* (U.S.A, Boston, Ticknor & fields, 1866)

Richter, Jean Paul, *Army Chaplain's Schmelzles Voyage to Flatz & Life of Quintus Fixlein* (Edinburgh & London: W.Tait & C. Tait, 1887)

Richter, Jean Paul, *Walt & Vult*, volume 1(U.S.A, Boston: Charles C, Little & James Brown, 1842)

Richter, Jean Paul, *The Moon* (in Holcraft, Richard, *Tales of Humour & Romance* (London: Longman, Rees, Orme, Brown & Green, 1829)

Richter, Jean Paul, *The Death of an Angel* (in Holcraft, Richard, *Tales of Humour &*

Romance (London: Longman, Rees, Orme, Brown & Green, 1829)

Richter, Jean Paul, *Reminiscences Of The Best Hours Of Life For The Hour Of Death*

(U.S.A, Boston: Joseph Dowe, 1841)

Richter, Jean Paul, *Sketches of and from Jean Paul,* (Oxford: A.W.Bennett, 1859)

The Jean Paul Society (http://www.jean-paul-gesellschft.de/.)

Secondary Sources:

Abrahams, Gerald, *The Age of Beethoven* (New York: Oxford University Press, 1982)

Ameriks Karl, *The Cambridge Companion to German Idealism* (Cambridge:

Cambridge University Press, 2000)

Appelbaum, Stanley, *Great German Poems of the Romantic Era* (NewYork: Dover

Publications, 1995

Attenhein Reckling Margarette, *Jean Paul's Reception in the Nineteenth and*

Twentieth Centuries (An Abridgment) (New York: The Graduate School of New York

University, 1938)

Austen, Jane, *Northanger Abbey (*London: Penguin, 1995)

Baker, Thomas Stockham, *Modern Language Notes* (Vol: xIii, No: 3)

Baldick, Chris, *Oxford Concise Dictionary of Eighteenth Century History* (London:

Basil Blackwell, 1994)

Balzac, Honore, De, *Eugenie Grandet* (Middlesex, Harmondsworth: Penguin, 1976)

Barnett, Corelli, *Bonaparte* (Hertfordshire: Wordsworth Military Library, 1997)

Becker Carl. L & Cooper Kenneth, S. *Europe since 1600: A Modern History* (London:

Burke Publishing Company Ltd, 1974)

Bennett, E.K, *A History of the German Novelle from Goethe to Thomas Mann* (Cambridge: Cambridge University Press, 1949)

Berger Dorothy, *Jean Paul Friedrich Richter* (New York: Twayne Publishers, 1972)

Berlin Isaiah, *The Roots of Romanticism* (Princeton & Oxford: Princeton University Press, 1999)

Bermann, Sandra, *Manzoni Alessandro: On the Historical Novel* (Lincoln & London: University of Nebraska Press, 1984)

Bevis, Matthew, *Comedy: A Very Short Introduction* (Oxford: Oxford University Press, 2013)

Black, J. Porter, *A Dictionary of Eighteenth Century History* (London: Basil Blackwell, 1994)

Blackall, Eric, A, *The Novels of the German Romantics* (U.S.A: Cornell University Press, 1983)

Blackstone, Bernard, *Byron: Literary Satire, Humour and Reflection* (Essex, Harlowe: Longman, 1971

Blamires, Harry, *The Age of Romantic Literature* (Essex: Longman, 1990)

Blanning, Tim, *The Romantic Revolution* (London: Weidenfeld & Nicolson, 2010)

Bondanella and Ciccarelli Amdrea, *The Cambridge Companion to the Italian Novel* (Cambridge: Cambridge University Press, 2003)

Börne Ludwig, The Crayon, Vol: 7, No: 11, November, 1860 (http://www.jstor.org/stable/25528132)

Botting, Fred, *Gothic* (London: Routledge, 1996)

Boyd, James, *Notes to Goethe's Poems, 1749 – 1786* (Oxford: Blackwell, 1966)

Boyd, William, *The Educational Theory of Jean-Jacques Rousseau* (New York: Russell & Russell, 1963)

Brand, Peter & Pertile, Lino, *The Cambridge History of Italian Literature*

(Cambridge: Cambridge University Press, 1996)

Brandes, George, *The French Romantics* (New York: Russell and Russell, 1966)

Brooks, T. C, The Crayon, Vol: 6, No: 4, (April 1859),

(http://www.jstor.org/stable/25527882)

Bygrave, Stephen, *Romantic Writings* (London: Routledge, 1996)

Carlyle, Thomas, *Critical & Miscellaneous Essays: Jean Paul Friedrich Richter-State

of German Literature-Life & Writings of Werner* (New York: John B. Alden, 1885)

Carlyle, Thomas, *German Romance: Specimens of its Chief Authors* (Oxford: Oxford

University Press, 1827)

Carlyle, Thomas, *German Romance: Translations from the German with

Biographical and Critical Notes* (London: Chapman & Hall, 1827)

Casey, Timothy, J, *Jean Paul: A Reader* (Baltimore & London: The John Hopkins

University Press, 1992)

Cecil, David, Lord, *The English Poets* (London: William Collins, 1941)

Charlton, D.G, France: *A Companion to French Studies* (London: Methuen, 1972)

Chateaubriand, Francoise-Rene, *Recollections of Italy, England and America with

Essays on Various Subjects, in Morals and Literature* (U.S.A, Philadelphia: M.Carey,

1816)

Christianson, Rupert, *Romantic Affinities: Portraits of an Age, 1780-1830*, (London:

Sphere Books, 1989)

Clarke, Kenneth, *The Gothic Revival* (London: John Murray, 1962)

Clayre, Alasdaire, *Nature and Industrialization* (Oxford: Oxford University Press, 1977)

Collins Easy Learn Dictionary (Glasgow: HarperCollins Publishers, 2006)

Collins, George Stuart, *Selections from the Works of Jean Paul Richter* (New York, Cincinnati, Chicago: American Book Company, 1899)

Crayon The, volume 3, No: 12, December 1856 (http://www.jstor.org/stable/25527882)

Crayon The, Volume 6, No: 4, April 1859 (http://www.jstor.org/stable/25527882)

Crayon The, Volume 7, No: 11, November 1860 (http://www.jstor.org/stable/25528132)

Cross, Maurice, *Selections from the Edinburgh Review, volume 2,* (France, Paris: Baudry's European Library, 1835)

Defoe, Daniel, *The Novels and Miscellaneous Works of Daniel Defoe: The History & Reality of Apparitions* (Oxford: London Talboys, 1840)

De Quincey, Thomas, *Essays on Philosophical Writers and Other Men of Letters, volume 1*(U.S.A, Boston: Ticknor Reed & Fields, 1853)

De Saussure, Necker, L.A. *Travels in Scotland: Descriptive State of Manners, Literature and Science* (London: Sir Richard Philips And Co,.1821)

Drabble, Margaret, *Oxford Companion to English Literature* (Oxford: Oxford University Press, 1985)

Durrani, Osmond, *German Poetry of the Romantic Era* (New York: Oswald Wolff, 1986)

Eagleton, Terry, *Literary Theory: An Introduction* (Oxford: Blackwell Publishing, Ltd, 1996)

Elton, Oliver, *A Survey of English Literature, 1780-1830, vol.1* (London: Edward Arnold, 1920)

Encyclopaedia Britannica, vol.2. (UK: Encyclopaedia Britannica, 1973)

Enright, D, J *The Oxford Book of Death* (Oxford: Oxford University Press, 1983)

Fichte, J.G. *Introductions to Wissenschafslehre 1797-1800* (U.S.A, Indianapolis: Hackett Publishing Company, Inc, 1994)

Fife, Herdon Robert. *Jean Paul Freidrich Richter & E.T.A Hoffmann* (PMLA Journal, volume 22, No: 1, 1907) (http://www.jstor.org/stable/450660)

Fleming, Paul, *The Pleasures of Abandonment: Jean Paul and the Life of Humour* (New York & Bonn: Konigshauen & Neumann, 2005)

Folkenflik, Vivian, *Major Writings of Germaine De Stael* (New York: Columbia University, 1987)

Frotheringham, Octavius Brooks, *Johann Gotflieb Fichte, 1762-1814* (http://www.alcott.net/alcott/home/champions/Fichte.html)

Furst, Lilian, *Romanticism* (London: Methuen, 1969)

Furst, Lilian, *Romanticism in Perspective* (London: Macmillan, 1969)

Garland, Henry & Garland Mary, *Oxford Companion to German Literature* (Oxford: Oxford University Press, 1976)

Gill, Stephen, *The Cambridge Companion to Wordsworth* (Cambridge: Cambridge University Press, 2003)

Gleckner, Robert F, *Romanticism: Points of View* (Englewood Cliffs, NJ: Prentice Hall, 1962)

Gostick, Joseph, *German Literature* (U.S.A, Philadelphia: Lippincott, Grambo & Co, 1854)

Halstead, John B, *Problems in European Civilization: Romanticism: Problems of Definition, Explanation and Evaluation* (U.S.A, Boston: D.C. Heath And Company, 1965)

Hardin, James, *Dictionary of Literary Biography, vol.90: German Writers in the Age of Goethe, 1789-1832*)

Hawley, Giles, *Wit, Wisdom & Philosophy of Jean Paul Friedrich Richter* (New York: Funk & Wagnalla, 1884)

Hazlitt, William, *Lectures on the Comic Writers*

Hereford, Charles, H, *The Age of Wordsworth* (London: Bell, 1914)

Herold, Christopher, J. *Mistress to An Age* (London: Readers Union, 1960)

Hill, Carl, *The Soul of Wit* (Lincoln & London: Nebraska University Press, 1993)

Hodgart, Matthew, *Satire* (London: Weidenfeld & Nicolson, 1969)

Holcraft, Richard, *Tales of Humour & Romance* (London: Longman, Rees, Orme, Brown and Green, 1829)

Holstein, Stael, Madame, De, *The Influence of Literature Upon Society, Volume 2* (U.S.A, Boston: W.Wells & T.B Wait & Co, 1813)

Hough, Graham, *The Romantic Poets* (London: Hutchinson University Library, 1858)

Howarth, W.D. Henri M. Peyre and John Cruickshank, *French Literature from 1660 to the Present* (London: Methuen & Co Ltd, 1974

Hughes, Glyn Tegai, *Romantic German Literature* (London: Edward Arnold, 1979)

Karl, R, Frederick, *A Reader's Guide to the Development of the English Novel in the Eighteenth Century* (London: Thames & Hudson, 1974)

Kipperman, Mark, *Beyond Enchantment: German Idealism & English Romantic Poetry* (Philadelphia: University of Pennsylvania Press, 1986)

Larrissy, Edward, *The Blind and Blindness in Literature of the Romantic Period* (Edinburgh: Edinburgh University Press, 2007)

Lefebure, Molly, *The Illustrated Lake Poets* (London: Tiger Books International, 1987)

Levene Leslie, *I THINK, THEREFORE I AM* (London: Michael O'Mara Books Ltd, 2013)

Levinson, Marjorie, *The Romantic Fragment Poem* (Chapel Hill & London: The University of North Carolina Press, 1986)

Lovejoy, Arthur, *Romanticism: Problems of Definition, Explanation & Evaluation* (Boston: D.C. Heath & Co, 1965)

Lytton, Edward Bulwer, *The Pilgrims of the Rhine* (London: Orion Books, 2010)

Maass, Joachim, *Kleist: A Biography* (London: Secker & Warburg, 1983)

Mason, Daniel Gregory, *The Romantic Composers* (London: MacMillan & Co, Ltd, 1906)

McDonald, Claudia, *Schumann's Piano Cycles and the Novels of Jean Paul* (Notes, 61, No: 3, 2005 (http://www.questia.comread/1P3-110386866)

McFarland, Thomas, *Romanticism & the Heritage of Rousseau* (Oxford: Clarendon Press, 1995)

Magill, C.P, *German Literature* (Lincoln: Oxford University Press, 1974)

Manzoni, Alessandro, *On the Historical Novel* (Lincoln & London: University of Nebraska Press, 1984)

Mason, Daniel Gregory, *The Romantic Composers* (London: MacMillan & Co, Ltd, 1906)

Menhennet, Alan, *The Romantic Movement* (London: Croom Helm Ltd, 1981)

Moore, Will, G, *French Achievement in Literature* (London: G.Bell and Sons, Ltd, 1969)

Morgan, Bayard, Quincy & Hohfeld, *German Literature in British Magazines, 1750-1860* (Madison, Wisconsin: University of Wisconsin Press, 1949)

Moser, Charles, *A Cambridge History of Russian Literature* (Cambridge: Cambridge University Press, 1989)

Neuburg, Victor E, *Popular Literature: A History and Guide* (London: The Woburn Press, 1977)

North Wind Journal of the George MacDonald Society

(http://www.ev90481.dial.pipex.com/gmsociety/nw14jeanpaul.htm)

North American Review volume 97, No: 200 July 1863

(http:/www.jstor.org/stable/25100382)

North American Review volume 99, No: 205 October, 1864

(http://www.jstor.org/stable/25100582)

Norton, Rictor, *Gothic Readings: The First Wave, 1764- 1840* (London: Leicester University Press, 2000)

O'Kelly, Helen, Watanabe, *The Cambridge History of German Literature* (Cambridge: Cambridge University Press, 1997)

Pfau, T, & Gleckner, R, *Lessons of Romanticism* (U.S.A: Duke University Press, 1998)

Pollard, Arthur, *Satire: The Critical Idiom* (London: Methuen & Co, Ltd, 1976)

Postgate, Helen, *Madam De Staël* (New York: Twayne Publishers, 1968)

Quernell, Peter, *Byron: The Years of Fame* (London: Collins, 1959)

Redekop, Benjamin, *Enlightenment and Community: Lessing, Abbt, Herder and the Quest for a German Public.* (Montreal: McGilt-Queens University Press, 2000)

Renwick, W.L, *English Literature 1789- 1815* (Oxford: Clarendon Press, 1963)

Ridge, George, Ross, *The Hero in French Romantic Literature* (U.S.A: University of Georgia Press, 1959)

Roe, Nicholas, *Romanticism* (Oxford: Oxford University Press, 2008)

Roe, Nicholas, *Romanticism in England* (Oxford: Oxford University Press, 2005)

Rolland, Romain, *French Thought in the Eighteenth Century: Rousseau, Voltaire, Diderot* (New York: David McKay, 1953)

Rolland, Romain, *Goethe and Beethoven* (New York, London: Benjamin Blom, 1968)

Rousseau, Jean-Jacques, *Thoughts on Different Subjects* (London: Crowder, Coote, Griffin and Locke, 1768)

Routh, J, & Wolff, J, (eds.) *The Sociology of Literature: Theoretical Approaches* (Staffordshire: Keele University, 1977)

Ryder, G, Frank, *German Romantic Novellas: Heinrich von Kleist and Jean Paul* (London & New York: Continuum, 1985)

Saintsbury, George, *A History of Nineteenth Century Literature, 1780 – 1895* (London: Macmillan And Co, 1896)

Samson, Jim, *The Cambridge History Of Nineteenth Century Music* (Cambridge: Clarendon Press, 1976)

Sampson, George, *The Concise Cambridge History of English Literature* (Cambridge: Cambridge University Press, 1946)

Smeed, J.W, *Jean Paul's Dreams* (Oxford: Oxford University Press, 1966)

Stahl, E.L, & Yuil, W.E, *German Literature in the 18th & 19th Centuries* (London: Cressett Press, 1970)

Stevens, David, *Romanticism* (Cambridge: Cambridge University Press, 2004)

Stockley, V, *German Literature As Known in England 1750 – 1800* (London: George Routledge, 1929)

Taggart, Caroline, *A Classical Education* (London: Michael O'Mara Books Limited, 2009)

Talmon, J.L, *Romanticism and Revolt: Europe 1815- 1848* (London: Thames & Hudson, 1967)

Terras, Victor, *A History of Russia* (New Haven & London: Yale University Press, 1991)

Thackeray, W.M, *The English Humorists of the Eighteenth Century* (Leipzig: Bernhard Tauchnitz, 1853)

Thayer Harvey.Waterman, *Laurence Sterne in Germany* (London: Dodo Press, 1905)

Tompkins, J.M.S, *The Popular Novel in England 1779- 1800* (London: Methuen, 1969)

Turnbull, Robert, *The Genius of Italy: Being Sketches of Italian Life, Literature & Religion* (London: David Bogue, 1849)

Vidler, Alec, R, *The Church in an Age of Revolution* (London: Penguin, 1990)

Waterhouse, Gilbert, *A Short History of German Literature* (London: Methuen, 1959)

Watt, Ian, *The Rise of the Novel* (London: The Hogarth Press, 1987)

Webb, William, *The North Wind Journal of the George MacDonald Society* (http://www.ev90481.dial.pipex.com_gmsociety/nw14_jeanpaul.html)

Webber A, *The Doppelganger: Double Visions in German Literature* (Oxford: Oxford University Press, 1996)

Wernaer Robert. M, *Romanticism and the German Romantic School* (http://www.jstor.org/stable/25106805)

Wheeler, Kathleen, M. *German Aesthetics and Literary Criticism* (Cambridge: Cambridge University Press, 1930)

Whyte, James, Arthur, *The Evolution of Modern Italy* (Oxford: Basil Blackwell, 1944)

Wilkinson, William Cleaver, *Classic German Course in English* (New York: Chautauqua Press, 1891)

Willoughby, L.A, *The Romantic Movement in Germany* (London: Oxford University Press, 1930)

Wright, David, (Ed.,), *The Penguin Book of English Romantic Verse* (Harmondsworth: Penguin, 1968)

Wu, Duncan, *Romanticism: An Anthology* (Oxford: Blackwell, 1994)

INDEX

*Nature,*7,8,9,10,11,14,15,17,20,22,24,25,27,28,31,32,37,39,40-43,46,48,51,53,54,59,60,61,65,67-69,71,73,74,77,79,83-86,88,89,92-94,101,119,124,126-132,136,139,140,146,147,151,155,156,157.